A Derbyshire Christmas

Derby Arboretum – winter 1890

A Derbyshire Christmas

Compiled by Robert Innes-Smith

ALAN SUTTON

First published in the United Kingdom in 1992 by
Alan Sutton Publishing Limited · Phoenix Mill · Far Thrupp
Stroud · Gloucestershire
in association with Derbyshire County Council · County Offices
Matlock · Derbyshire

First published in the United States of America in 1992 by
Alan Sutton Publishing Inc · 83 Washington Street
Dover NH 03820

Reprinted 1993

British Library Cataloguing in Publication Data

Derbyshire Christmas
I. Innes-Smith, Robert
820.8033

ISBN 0-7509-0073-3

Library of Congress Cataloging in Publication Data applied for

Cover illustration: Winter's day *(photograph: Fine Art Photographic Library Ltd)*

Typeset in Garamond 12/13.
Typesetting and origination by
Alan Sutton Publishing Limited.
Printed in Great Britain by
WBC, Bridgend, Mid Glam.

Contents

Christmas in Derbyshire

The following is an extract from the Journal of the Derbyshire Archaeological Society *1852, Vol. VII, p. 206.*

Christmas festivities are well observed in Derbyshire; mummers or guisers go from house to house, and perform a play of St George. They are dressed up in character and decorated with ribands, tinsel, and other finery, and on being admitted into the house commence their performance by St George announcing himself by beginning his oration:

I am St George, the noble champion bold,
And with my glittering sword
I've won three crowns of gold;
It's I who fought the fiery dragon,
And brought it to the slaughter;
And so I won the fair Sabra,
The King of Egypt's daughter,
– Seven have I won, but married none,
And bear my glory all alone,
– And with my Sword in my hand,
Who dare against me stand?
I swear I'll cut him down
With my victorious brand.

Derbyshire winter landscape

A champion is soon found in the person of Slasher who accepts the challenge. St George then replies in a neat speech, when they sing, shake hands, and fight with their wooden swords, and Slasher is slain. The King then enters, saying 'I am the King of England, the greatest man alive,' and after walking round the dead body, calls for 'Sir Guy, one of the chiefest men in the world's wonder,' who shows his wonderful courage and prowess in calling for a doctor. The doctor, on making his appearance, gives a long and quaint account of his

birth, parentage, education, and travels, whilst perambulating around the fallen Slasher, and ends his oration by saying:

> Here take a little out of my bottle,
> And put it down thy throttle.

The dead man is thus cured, and having received the advice of 'Rise, Jack, and fight again,' the play is ended.

A Bunch of Snowdrops

SIR OSBERT SITWELL, Bt.

Sir Osbert Sitwell, Bt., OM, was one of the greatest masters of English prose of the twentieth century. The elder son of Sir George Sitwell, Bt., and brother of Dame Edith Sitwell and Sir Sacheverell Sitwell, Bt., he spent much of his life at Renishaw Hall in north Derbyshire and in his Italian castle of Montegufoni in Tuscany.

Like his brother and sister, Sir Osbert was a poet, but his chief claim to fame is as a writer of prose and, in particular, his five-volumed autobiography Left Hand, Right Hand! *'A Bunch of Snowdrops' first appeared in the* Sunday Times *in the 1940s. It must be one of the most poignant evocations of Christmas ever written.*

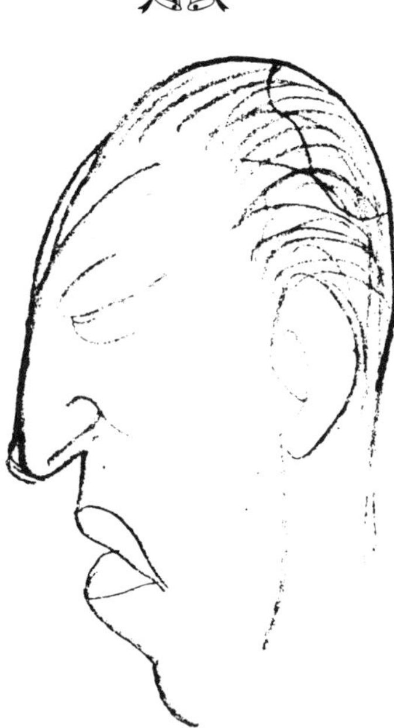

Sir Osbert Sitwell from a sketch by Sir Max Beerbohm in the Editor's collection

For those who are no longer children, Christmas, whether they enjoy it or not, must inevitably be a brief period of nostalgia. The eve of Christmas some years ago I spent in the house of my two dearest friends in Boston and in the atmosphere of pervading hospitality and affection which they evoked all feelings of sadness were quickly forgotten . . . Only in the darkness of the night, when I woke up, a sudden scent of snowdrops assailed me, and it seemed to me suddenly that I had come a long and tiring way from the point at which I started.

As I lay there in the darkness the Christmases I had spent in my childhood loomed up at me like beads on a chain, or snowdrops gathered in a bunch . . . The first I remember was spent under the hospitable roof of Ganton, the country

'. . . for ever in my memory against a background of snow'

house of the Legards in Yorkshire, and a name known to all lovers of memoirs because of its frequent occurrence in the pages of the Comtesse de Boigne's reminiscences. Sir Charles Legard, portly and affable in the manner of the Prince of Wales (for we are still in Queen Victoria's reign), wearing a bowler hat and a dark suit, and Lady Legard, my godmother, tight-waisted, charitable, dressed in lilac and white, are drawn for ever in my memory against a background of snow. There was a famous frost that winter, and they were forced to walk delicately when they went out, as if walking on ropes – and I remember that the cold had obliged the rabbits to nibble every morsel of stick or leaf above the snow level.

The memory is sweet, tender and bitter as the smell of the first bunches of snowdrops, which reached us when we returned to our house nearby at Scarborough; and which remain for me ever associated with the festival. As they lay there, before my nurse took them from their damp box, I well remember my rapture at seeing those delicate, green-veined, frosty flowers, gothic in shape and edged with green, and with particularly evasive and enticing scent; indeed, invented for what reason, except to please human beings, because assuredly no insects are present at that season to be attracted?

'. . . as if walking on ropes'

After the first festival to be recalled, when I was three or four, came a Christmas spent in London . . . I entered enthusiastically into the idea. It meant, I know, that we should be taken on the night of Boxing Day to the opening of the Christmas pantomime at Drury Lane – an occasion for which all children longed – and see the great Dan Leno as the Widow Twankey in 'Aladdin'.

And, indeed, the atmosphere of London at Christmas did prove overwhelming: the moment we reached the station, after a journey of five unheated hours, it came at us. The station was a cavern of iron, with a glass roof, full of the fog and smoke of aeons: from its menacing, dark shelter, full of shouts and bustle, we stepped into a four-wheeler, bitterly cold, and smelling of oats, beer and fog in equal proportions. Even the hoarse voice of the rednosed cabman carried out, as it were, the same stupendous summary of the season.

We drove to Grosvenor Square, where was the family mansion, and in it an exotic air of warmth, excitement and Christmas delights and surprises; which prevailed, too, in the

daytime in the nearby streets of shops, in the bouquets of sweet-scented flowers in the windows, bright as coloured sugars, in the toy-shops, crowded with ingenious mechanical treasures, and the fruit shops, now full of tangerines, southern fruits, Elvas plums, starred with coloured paper, dates and raisins. Down Bond Street and Piccadilly drove the elegant carriages, and the hansoms, shell-like and brittle and polished, the black gondolas of the London streets. The size of London, in its thick muffling canopy of white or yellow fog, was immense, imposing: a fog lit by flares and torches, and through its often impenetrable texture would sound perpetually the cheerful, faintly contaminated cockney vowels, as the shoppers at stalls and small stores called, one to another, and spoke of the weather, and of Christmas.

Yet, in spite of that urban experience of it, Christmas remains for me essentially a rural feast. Only a few Christmases did we spend at Renishaw – and these were overshadowed by my father's disapproval of the whole occasion, and by his fear of 'getting the children into extravagant habits by giving them presents'. (He hated to give presents to people who expected them, or when they expected them, and I still recall, with some tremors of discomfort, the Christmas I spent with him in Venice some 30 years ago, and how, when the amiable Italian waiter remarked to him 'Good morning, Sir George, and a happy Christmas!' he replied in a tone of disillusioned comprehension, 'I know!')

My mother certainly made up for our lack of amusements as much as she could; yet Christmas at home remained a rather barren festival. But when I was about eight, my grandfather died and we began to spend Christmas every year in the house of his son. And it was the series of ten or so Christmases, spent under the roof of my uncle and aunt Londesborough at Blankney, that have subsequently conditioned and defined my ideas of Christmas, its horrors and pleasures.

Renishaw Hall in Sir Osbert Sitwell's time

It was perhaps not a typical Christmas, being more international and exotic, and scarcely Christian, except for brief desultory, purely formal appearances in church. The large house was always full of relatives of every age, from second childhood down to first: some were in bathchairs, others in perambulators, some remembered King George IV and the great Duke of Wellington, some remembered nothing, from having left off remembering, others had not yet begun to remember. There would often be foreign connections present as well as English.

As for the children, except for the presence of my father – who, as I have explained, played an opposite role, and was, in any case, intensely unpopular, as the only man of studious bent and, indeed, of real intelligence present in the gathering – we were tied to compulsory pleasure, as later, at school to compulsory games. We took part certainly in the feasting of our elders. We

watched them hunting, shooting, and engaged in other diverse and repulsive sports, but we were, on the other hand, made to perform a French play, under the tuition of a whole platoon of governesses. This would be given before villagers who understood no word of French, and were there by a kind of *corvée*.

But, above all, Christmas was henceforth to be associated for me with my giant and genial uncle and his passions for music and mechanics. In the passages he had accumulated some 12 or 14 mechanical organs; cases with glass fronts that revealed trumpets and drums that, when set in motion, could be seen indulging in an orgy of self-blowing and self-beating. This elementary, if expensive, form of juke-box greatly pleased the children, even if it exacerbated the nerves of our elders, who did not like their favourite selections from Verdi – for such they usually were – played in this fashion.

Renishaw Hall from the garden

But now the music is stilled, the machines are obsolete; the fashionable beauties and the plain, poor relations are equally unfashionable, for they are dead, even most of these who were young children 50 years ago – and the dead are always unfashionable. The strong, tall men are forgotten, the sports in which they indulged are dying. But as I look back, I see the vast tents of the rooms, lighted during the day's dark as well as the night's, shining out for miles over untrodden fields of snow that ended beyond our vision in the white-fringed sea; rooms that were filled with the contemporary symbols of luxury, palm trees of exceptional stature, poinsettias that seemed to bear as flowers stars cut out of red flannel; a fragrance of wood-smoke, and jonquils, lilac and freesias, hangs in the air. But, framing all these and bringing them back to me, is the more rustic smell of snowdrops, edged with a few prickly green leaves, their stalks tied roughly, inexpertly with thin, damp string, lying in a damp cardboard box that has just been opened.

'. . . lying in a damp cardboard box that has just been opened'

Ghosts, Spectres and Ghouls of Derbyshire

ROSSLYN ST CLAIR

Rosslyn St Clair is a nom-de-plume *of a well-known Derbyshire writer and journalist.*

Phantom coaches, headless women, cold clammy kisses and a dramatic and mysterious mass resurrection are all part of the psychical lore of Derbyshire, yet on the face of it the county does not seem over blessed (or cursed, depending on how you look at it) with these phenomena. Essex has its Borley Rectory, County Meath in Ireland has its phantom foxes of Gormanston; Angus in Scotland has its ghostly drummer of Cortachy and the numerous spectres of Glamis; the Tower of London has Anne Boleyn – the list of famous ghosts is endless, but one is hard pressed to think of any famous Derbyshire shades. It is only when one delves a little that all the nasties and ghastlies are uncovered and Derbyshire, after all, turns out to have its fair share of ghosts of every kind.

'I saw the figure with such distinctness that I had no doubt at all that I was looking at a real person,' wrote Lady Ida

Sitwell. She had been to a local charity ball, had returned home to Renishaw late at night and was resting on a sofa in the upstairs drawing room before retiring. Suddenly the figure of a woman with grey hair, who looked as if she might have been a servant, appeared. She was wearing a blue dress, a dark shawl and a white cap and she glided to the top of what was once a staircase and disappeared. Lady Ida's husband, Sir George Sitwell, ever ready with an explanation, wrote that such apparitions 'Were not ghosts but phantasms, reversed impressions of something seen in the past and now projected from an over tired and excited brain', ending with the paradoxical statement, 'ghosts are sometimes met with but are not ghosts'.

Miss Tait, a relative of the Sitwells and daughter of a former Archbishop of Canterbury, Dr Campbell Tait, told the ghost-hunting Lord Halifax another story about Renishaw. She was staying there once in a certain room and was awakened by three cold kisses.The terrified woman rushed to the bedroom of Miss Florence Sitwell, the sister of her host Sir George, where she spent the rest of the night. The next day, when the Agent, Mr Turnbull, was told this story, he confirmed that the same thing had happened to a friend of his who had once slept in that room. Later, during alterations, an empty coffin was found under the floorboards of the room.

It is a Sunday evening in Chesterfield, on the 24th January 1674 to be precise. An elderly and worthy couple of the town have retired to bed and are asleep. Just before 3 a.m. they are awakened by the sound of frantic knocking on the bedroom door. The man jumps from his bed and opens the door. He reels back with terror for standing there is '. . . A Dog of great Stature, cole black colour, and most terrible to behold, which presently vanished away with many horrible howlings and screechings . . .' Petrified and shaken the man calls a constable but nothing is found.

The next evening a similar knocking occurred. This time 'a woman's shape, all bloody' stood before them and then vanished to the accompaniment of blood-curdling sounds.

The next day the old couple were visibly shaken but they were nevertheless prepared when, on the following night, a similar knocking was heard. On opening the door the man beheld a stranger of enormous stature standing in the doorway. He spoke in a quiet, kindly way and asked the old man to accompany him. The latter courageously followed the spectre to a field not far away, and was shown a hoard of money. The ghost explained that it had lived a wicked life and had stolen the money. It bid the old man to take it and return it to its rightful owners, and then vanished. The old man took the money and distributed it to those from whom it had been stolen. An account of this strange occurrence was published very soon afterwards and the names of four witnesses were given. These included two constables and a churchwarden.

Duffield has a traditional phantom coach with skeleton coachmen and postilions and five white horses with fiery eyes and smoking nostrils. This nightmarish apparition used to be seen regularly rushing along the Valley of the Derwent and as it approached Duffield Bridge, it dashed into the river and disappeared.

Chaddesden was once described as 'prolific in stories of the supernatural' and used to boast two headless women who could be encountered at night sitting on stiles. They were not connected and appeared in different parts of the vicinity. On the main road between Chaddesden and Derby a waggon and horses were often seen dashing along through an adjacent field with 'an old infernal driver'. This spectral vehicle was also said to snap up the unwary straggler who would never be seen again.

Derbyshire can, perhaps, claim the most extraordinary story of all time; a story which will probably remain the strangest

even until the crack of doom. It is recounted by Dr James Clegg, a worthy, down-to-earth, non-conformist minister of Chapel-en-le-Frith. As might be guessed by his pre-fix Dr Clegg was a man of some learning and was the author of *The Life of the Rev John Ashe*, a biography of the religious writer and dissenting minister of Ashford who died in 1735.

In a letter dated 1754 this worthy minister described to a fellow clergyman the fantastic occurrence which took place in the churchyard at Hayfield. It so happened that there was a large communal grave there and one day in late August of that year, in the presence of numerous spectators, the grave opened and several hundred bodies emerged and ascended towards Heaven singing in concert. They wore no winding sheets nor were they naked but 'their vesture seemed streaked with gold, interlaced with sable and skirted with white'.

'Several hundred bodies emerged and ascended towards Heaven'

Those who witnessed this extraordinary mass resurrection must have thought that Doomsday had arrived, but as a later writer cynically put it, no doubt with tongue in cheek, that it must have been gratifying to the local inhabitants to see their forefathers all going upwards in the right direction!

Moor Farm Sporting Club in Flash Lane, Darley Dale, was once a popular modernised establishment with little hint of its gruesome past. Centuries ago it was a lonely wayside inn which had a very peculiar landlady with Sweeney Todd tendencies. She had a habit of murdering unsuspecting travellers who stopped for sustenance and shelter. They ended up a in great stone coffin in the cellar. This sadistic lady had a horrible end herself. Having been found out she was hanged *and* beheaded, and her ghost was long reputed to haunt the place. In recent times the building was destroyed by fire and has been rebuilt as a private house.

Renishaw is not by any means the only haunted country house in Derbyshire. Barlborough Hall has its Grey Lady and another female of the same colour haunts the Old Hall Farm at Youlgreave, while in the Hall itself ghostly clashing swords have been heard in one of the bedrooms known as the Duel Room where a Cavalier and a Roundhead are reputed to have fought to the death one dark November night. The fight is said to be re-enacted on the anniversary. Taddington Hall has two spectres, one the ghost of a victim of fratricide, the other the shade of a drunken farmer who was in the habit of rolling home tipsy on market days. One day, to the amazement of his wife, he rolled in through the door without opening it and vanished. Afterwards it was learnt that he had fallen off his horse and killed himself.

Highlow Hall has the reputation of being one of the most haunted houses in the county and was actually featured on television one Christmas in a programme on ghosts. The house was for long the property of the ancient Derbyshire

Youlgreave Hall – where the ghostly clashing of swords is heard

Highlow Hall – one of the most haunted houses in Derbyshire

family of Eyre. One owner, Robert Eyre, was extremely bad tempered and is said to have run through with his sword two workmen engaged in enlarging the house. One he caught dicing when he should have been working, the other he overheard grumbling about him. Both victims are among Highlow's ghosts.

There are many other stories of hauntings and spectres in Derbyshire like the 'Fairie Dogge' of the Peak, the haunted barn at Shatton and the Magic Huntsman of Bretton Clough, but these are tales for another time.

Christmas in the Olden Time at Haddon Hall

Haddon Hall is one of the most romantic-looking houses in England. It escaped all the architectural fashions and survived the centuries little changed from when it was first completed. It is a seat of the Dukes of Rutland, but before that it belonged to the Vernon family from whom the dukes descend through the female line.

Sir George Vernon, known as 'The King of the Peak', was the last of his line to own Haddon. In his day, when the Tudors

Haddon Hall at the time of Sir George Vernon

reigned, he gained his soubriquet by the magnificence of his entertaining and his lavish hospitality. He was lord of thirty manors and it does not take much imagination to view in the mind's eye the Christmas splendours presided over by Sir George at Christmas time in Haddon's Great Hall and Long Gallery.

Here is a letter sent to 'Local Notes and Queries', a fortnightly column in the Derbyshire Times *(22 December 1872) by Reginald W. Corlass.*

In Nash's *Mansions of England in the olden time* there is a plate depicting the Banqueting Hall, at Haddon, which is rather interesting, from the fact of its giving some idea of the way in which Christmas was spent by our forefathers. It is a scene well worthy of a time, when, whatever may have been the condition of society in other respects, the people entered with

Christmas revelry at Haddon Hall in Tudor times

a real and hearty enjoyment into their pleasures. Around on the walls of the spacious apartment are hung boughs of evergreens, suits of armour, gay banners and trophies of the chase; and the Yule log is roaring in the deep, old-fashioned fireplace. At the right is a large oak table, on which stand beakers of ale and refreshments, and a merrymaker is mounted upon it, with outstretched cup toasting the players in the gallery, each of whom seems bent upon making his particular instrument the most heard. Here also in the entrance, stand the Lord and his guests, watching the merrymaking of his retainers and their friends.

The centre of the floor is occupied by a most motley group. In the foreground four jesters, with bells on every portion of their dress, are executing a kind of jig, hand in hand; whilst behind stalks a ferocious looking giant, the head and upper part of whom is formed of wood, surmounted by three long white feathers, and holding in his hand an enormous wooden scimitar. Close by him, advancing with a huge club, is a wild man covered with long hair or fur; and entering in at one of the doors, amongst a crowd of dependents carrying torches and flagons, are the figures of a griffin and a knight, whose shield bears the cross of St George, in full armour riding a hobby horse. In the foreground is a large scaly crocodile, between the wide open jaws of which can be seen the head of the man inside, who is vainly attempting to progress across the hall on all-fours, a companion laughingly holding him back by his long flexible tail. Astride of this last masker sits a page waving small flags.

Those who are not taking part in the masquerade are gathered in the corners, drinking or smoking among themselves, or looking on at the mummers. One old man, whose bent limbs betoken a tendency to rheumatism, number one being evidently predominant in his thoughts, is stirring up the faggots to a blaze with a severe countenance, regardless of the fun

The Long Gallery at Haddon

going on around him; whilst a jolly old couple, the girth of whose waists and contented looks speak volumes for the character of their master, have evidently, to judge from the broad grins which overspread their sleek features, given themselves up, mind and body, to thorough enjoyment. In the deep recess of one of the high windows, a young swain is struggling with a pretty, half-reluctant maid, to impress upon her tempting lips the sweet punishment incurred by being found beneath the 'mistletoe bough' whether wilfully or not, who can say? Such was the scene enacted no doubt in many a hall and mansion throughout England, at this merry season of the year, in olden days.

The times have changed, and we have changed with them, and though perhaps nowadays less heartiness and sincerity pervade our social intercourse, we have lost much of the sensuality and rudeness of the middle ages, and now enjoy in a more rational and refined manner, what I wish to one and all of my readers – 'A Merry Christmas and a Happy New Year'.

A Christmas Letter from Lord Chesterfield

Philip Dormer Stanhope, 4th Earl of Chesterfield (1694–1773) was the head of two out of the three main branches of the Stanhope family who were seated in Derbyshire. The Earls of Harrington (see page 128) lived at Elvaston Castle, near Derby and the Chesterfields had Bretby Hall which, in its time, rivalled Chatsworth as one of the most sumptuous houses in the county. Chesterfield, who spent much of his time in London, wrote a series of letters to his illegitimate son full of good advice and exhortations. When his son died, he continued his letters in much the same vein to his cousin who was also his godson and eventual heir, another Philip.

Dr Johnson said that the letters 'teach the morals of a whore and the manners of a dancing master' – but then Johnson was heavily biased against Chesterfield for reasons that are well known. These letters were written to his great friend Solomon Dayrolles, his godson and secretary, who was Ambassador to The Hague for a time.

The 4th Earl of Chesterfield

To Solomon Dayrolles, Esq.

Bath, Christmas-day, 1757

Dear Dayrolles,

I have, this moment, received your letter. I firmly believe the King of Prussia's victory* at Lissa; the account of it, to and from the two Mitchels,† must, I think, upon the whole be true, though perhaps magnified in particular parts. I am very glad of it; but soberly so, for, to give me joy, I must have a great deal more. If there has been a battle in the Electorate, I

* Over the Austrians commanded by Prince Charles of Lorraine. This battle, fought on 5 December, exactly one month after Rosbach, was at first called Lissa from the name of the neighbouring woods, but has since derived its appellation from the village of Leuthen. Napoleon speaks of it as *un chef d'œuvre de mouvements, de manœuvres et de résolution*. (*Mémoires* publiés par Montholon, vol. v. p. 215.)

† Sir Andrew Mitchel, the British Envoy to the Prussian Court; and Mr Mitchel, for many years Resident from the King of Prussia in England – Dayrolles' Note.

will venture to prophesy that those who attacked got the better; for I suppose that Monsieur de Richelieu would be wise enough not to risk a battle without a great superiority, and in that case, if he attacked, I fear we shall be beaten; but, if he found himself in a situation in which he could not avoid a battle, and that we attacked him, I think we shall beat him. But, if we do, still mark the end on't.

The more I think over the three plans mentioned in my last, the more I think them both necessary and practicable. This, at least, I am sure of, that they are our last convulsive struggles, for at this rate we cannot possibly live through the year 1759. *Nous jouons de notre reste*, and therefore should push it, *à toute outrance.*

As for the House of Lords, I may say with truth, What is Hecuba to me, or I to Hecuba? What can I do in that numerous assembly, who cannot enjoy the company of three or four

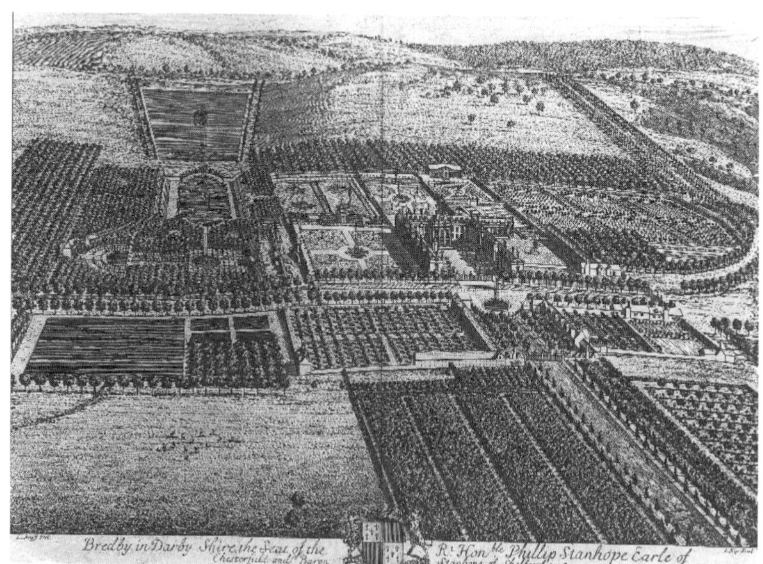

Bretby, the Derbyshire seat of Lord Chesterfield, long since demolished

friends by the chimney corner or round a table? Can I, or should I, speak, when I cannot reply? No; quiet is both my choice and my lot. The will must now stand for the deed; I shall sincerely wish well to my species, to my country, and to my friends, but can serve none of them. What little offices I can do in private life, I will to my power.

This is the season of compliments, consequently of lies; I will therefore make you none at such a suspicious time. You know I love you, Mrs Dayrolles, and all who belong to you both; guess the rest.

Yours faithfully

Christmas Day in the Workhouse – 1890

It is Christmas Day in the Workhouse,
  And the cold bare walls are bright
With garlands of green and holly,
  And the place is a pleasant sight:
For with clean-washed hands and faces,
  In a long and hungry line
The paupers sit at the tables
  For this is the hour they dine.

George R. Sims

The following is a report from an Ashbourne newspaper.

Christmas 1890 will long be remembered by the inmates of the Union Workhouse. True philanthropy generates in the bosom of its possessor a feeling of delight when he beholds his fellow men participating in passing pleasures. Christmas at the Workhouse this year, as for some years past, was a time of festivity and gladness. In the morning of Christmas Day in the chapel, which was plainly but neatly decorated, the simple Church Service was gone through with much heartiness by the numerous inmates, the children leading the singing, and the Revd F. Jourdain, the Vicar's son, officiating.

This over, all the inmates, except those who were confined to the sick wards, made their way to the dining hall, where a feast awaited them, the sight of which brought a bright smile of Christmas joy to every face. The abundant supply of good old English roast beef, of prime quality, about 120 lb. from Mr Shakespeare's, and good plum pudding soon yielded to the keen appetites of the inmates.

The sentiment conveyed in the second sentence of this report, would, we feel, have been the experience of any philanthropist who might have witnessed the gusto with which about 60 inmates partook of the good cheer which was provided without the least stint. The inmates were waited on by a Guardian and his daughter, the Master and Matron, Mr Cave (the porter), and other members of the household staff. To the oft-repeated query, 'Have you had enough?' the answer, 'Yes, thank you,' was given. As one looked on the busy scene, the choice adornment of the table, and as one watched the happy inmates enjoying the Guardians' hospitality one could not help offering silent congratulations that the Board had thought fit to provide them such a capital meal. It was a cheery sight to see the old men and women in their neat and clean, though rather quaint, costume, sitting smilingly

The Ashbourne Union Workhouse in 1848 drawn by B.H. Sadler

around the festive board and wishing one another, 'A Happy Christmas.'

The invalids and those too infirm to unite with the rest were not uncared for or forgotten; they received every kindness and attention befitting such a joyous season, and doubtless, as far as their infirmities would allow them, they, too, enjoyed a bright Christmas. Before leaving the room, cheers were given for the Guardians, and also for Mr E.S. and Miss Bradley, who had kindly assisted at the dinner. The Master feelingly reciprocated their kind wishes. He thanked Mr and Miss Bradley, on behalf of the inmates for their presence and kind service, and to their thoughtful friends who had been good enough to send gifts. The inmates were very thankful. Mr Bradley made a few encouraging and suitable remarks, to which the inmates paid earnest heed. By this time Mr A. Tuthill had arrived. Preparation was now made for further

enjoyment. That universal solace, tobacco, was served out to the men. Oranges, nuts, sweets, &c., were also handed round to the inmates, and both young and old appeared to be having a jolly time of it. Snuff and other modicums were freely distributed amongst the inmates.

Later in the day the boys gave a nigger burlesque, the old men sang songs recalling to memory scenes of long ago, and in the evening a party of carol singers, 18 in number, under the charge of Mr James Avery, gave a vocal entertainment. The room was most gaily decorated for the occasion with the usual ornaments used in Christmas decorations and presented quite a fairy like appearance. The decorations and mottoes caused a transformation, and in short festoons and devices were abundant. Mottoes of a consoling and comforting nature were placed all around the room. They were worked in red letters on a white ground with a border of green which gave it a pretty effect. They were executed and designed by the Master, who takes a delight in making glad the hearts of the inmates at such times.

We cannot conclude our account of 'Christmas at the Workhouse' without commending the energetic Master and Matron, Mr and Mrs F. Wilkinson. By their efforts the dull life which might otherwise be spent in the house is greatly cheered and brightened, and visitors cannot but be struck with the very neat and happy appearance of the seniors, and the good behaviour of the children. Altogether, the Ashbourne Union Workhouse is not such a bad place after all in which to spend Christmas, and we cannot help thinking that many a poor family outside spent a far less happy one.

The Mike-Shy Ghost

KENNETH BIRD

The ambition of every producer and outside broadcast commentator is to introduce listeners at Christmas-time to a real, live ghost. A talking ghost, for preference, or even one with a blood-curdling laugh.

We, who work for the BBC, know that listeners like nothing better than to be scared out of their wits as midnight draws near, and the day's festivities give way to pleasant relaxation before a dying fire. Each year, we scratch our heads and search through books of historical research in the hope that we shall come across a ghost with 'a microphone manner.'

Alas, ghosts that are audible are few and far between. In Derbyshire, for instance, we can trace innumerable 'grey ladies' and 'headless knights' but their stock-in-trade seems to be an eerie silence. Some of us are bitter about this, we feel that they are seeking the glamour of a television screen rather than the, perhaps, more limited delights of sound broadcasting.

It is no use for a commentator to describe the appearance of a ghost. His teeth may chatter, his hair may bristle like the quills of a hedgehog, but the listener, secure at his fireside, is unconvinced. Today there is little belief in ghostly manifestations.

Many attempts have been made by commentators to describe a ghost. They have crouched in moonlit corridors surrounded by recording gear, waiting, waiting . . . but never once has anything appeared.

It was in Derbyshire, one Christmas before the war, that a BBC commentator had a rather curious experience. Don't ask me exactly where it happened – I don't know, and the man concerned is now in Australia. If I remember rightly, it was in a large manor house in or near the Peak district that the ghost hunt was staged.

The commentator was waiting for one of those rare manifestations – a ghost whose footsteps could be heard coming along a corridor. The footsteps were loud and dragging – in the best 'ghost story' tradition.

A microphone was placed in the corridor, while the commentator sat with another in the ballroom, where, according to several eye-witnesses, the ghost was supposed to appear as a headless cavalier.

Suddenly, the footsteps were heard . . . then they ceased. The commentator dashed over to the engineer in the next room and asked if he had recorded the footsteps all right. 'Course I haven't,' snapped the engineer, 'you'd switched off the mike.' The commentator denied it, but sure enough the microphone in the corridor had not only been switched off but disconnected.

Both commentator and engineer swear that that microphone was connected when they left it. They'd checked and double-checked it. They connected it again, but no more footsteps were heard that night – or any other night.

So you see – we at the BBC are rather disillusioned about ghosts.

from

A Derbyshire Year – December

ELIZABETH EISENBERG

Elizabeth Eisenberg is Derbyshire born and bred. After retiring from her career as a schoolmistress she took to writing on local Derbyshire topics and has had several books published in the Derbyshire Heritage Series. In 1977 she won the Derbyshire Festival Story Competition for a piece in the local dialect and she has twice won a scholarship to the Derbyshire National Writers' School. She has written two village histories including one on Wingerworth where she was born.

ROYALTY IN DERBYSHIRE

On December 4th, 1745, the county had the doubtful honour of a 'Royal Visit' when Bonnie Prince Charlie, the Young Pretender, on his way to London to claim the English throne, rode into Derby market place accompanied by lifeguards playing bagpipes.

Wearing tartan dress and an elaborately trimmed bonnet, the Prince was escorted to Exeter House where he was accommodated for the night while his rebel army of followers, famished and lice-ridden, were billeted with the townspeople to

Exeter House, Derby, where Prince Charles Edward Stuart stayed in 1745

the depletion of their cellars and larders. Forty-three soldiers occupied No. 28 Irongate, the house where Joseph Wright, the artist, was born in 1734. The family, like many others, had moved out for safety.

On December 6th, having decided to abandon 'this irresponsible enterprise', as Sir Winston Churchill described it, the Prince sent an advance guard to establish a bridgehead at Swarkestone while he made his retreat, his disgruntled army commandeering horses, carts and a great deal of produce as they marched through Ashbourne on their way north.

DECEMBER 21ST IS THE FEAST OF SAINT THOMAS, THE APOSTLE

This was the day on which poor people went round their villages 'Thomassing', called in some parts of Derbyshire 'Going a-Mumping'. Women and children called at the houses

of better-off parishioners and begged either money or food for Christmas. At any other time of the year, begging was looked upon as a disgrace but was considered acceptable on St Thomas's day everywhere in England and the contributions made all the difference to the way in which poverty stricken families could celebrate Christmas.

Candles, cheese or bags of flour were the customary gifts and farmers were expected to give potatoes or wheat. The latter was ladled out of a sack into cans or basins and used to make frumenty for breakfast on Christmas morning. In return, the donors were presented with a sprig of holly for luck.

In Duffield, boys and girls used bolster slips or made long narrow bags of cloth. In these they collected dry goods like oatmeal, sugar or rice which was put into the bag and tied round with string before adding the offering from the next house. This was fastened in the same way until the bag resembled a length of sausages.

It was said that Quarndon householders never gave more than a few apples for a Thomassing present while people in Hazelwood parish complained to the teachers that throughout the day children came knocking at their door calling, 'A Happy Saint Thomas's Day' when they should have been in school.

At Breadsall, there is still a sum of money from a charity set on one side to be distributed among the needy on St Thomas's Day.

December 24th is Christmas Eve, the day on which Christmas cards used to be posted in the certainty that they would be delivered on Christmas morning.

The Yule Log was carried into the house, though not until dusk and set in an open hearth. A piece of holly was arranged behind each picture.

The Posset Bowl, its contents a mixture of warm milk spiced with nutmeg and ale to make it curdle, was put on the table for visitors to ladle out a helping for themselves.

Boys and girls who had taken the parts of Mary and Joseph, angels and shepherds and wise men in the school Nativity Play, now exchanged clothes with each other. Girls wearing boys' caps back to front and boys in bonnets and aprons set off round their villages to sing carols while mothers stuffed the turkeys.

One verse of 'While Shepherds Watched' at each door in north Derbyshire was followed by,

> Hole in me stocking, hole in me shoe,
> Please will you give me a copper or two.
> If yer haven't a penny, a ha'penny will do,
> If yer haven't a ha'penny, God bless you.'

At Wensley and Winster, frightening figures wearing grotesque masks went from house to house demanding money or food without, as one report commented, 'making the least effort to render any kind of hymn or carol.'

South of Derby, the singing usually opened with 'Good King Wenceslas', king and page being sung by individual voices. Then in loud unison came the 'Yuletide Blessing':

> A merry, merry Christmas,
> A Happy New Year,
> A pocket full of money,
> A cellar full of beer
> And a good fat pig to kill next year.

At one time most parishes had a team of handbell ringers. Their carol playing on Christmas Eve was very popular and attracted a crowd of people who followed them round the village and sang to their accompaniment.

'A green Yule makes a fat churchyard.'

DECEMBER 26TH IS SAINT STEPHEN'S DAY

St Stephen was the first Christian to be martyred for his faith and was put to death by stoning.

It used to be the day for making gifts to the poor. Food, clothes and money were given from church funds to people in need and many individuals gave away the remains of their Christmas dinners and looked in their clothes closets to see which of their garments could be discarded in the name of charity.

This day is also called BOXING DAY, probably because it was the day on which alms boxes in churches were opened and the contents distributed to the poor of the parish.

Farmers' wives in Derbyshire made huge meat pies which they cut up and sent to the families of their farm labourers.

In 1762 the Duke of Devonshire received a Boxing Day gift from a friend in Yorkshire. It was a gigantic pie which contained pheasants, turkeys, plovers, snipe, woodcock, partridge and a hare. After supplying a meal for the family at Chatsworth it was given, in portions, on Boxing Day evening to the outdoor servants.

December 26th has always been a popular time for meets of hounds in Derbyshire, like the annual turnout at Kedleston Hall.

Saint Stephen was regarded as the patron saint of horses and this day was the original date fixed for the bloodletting of horses and working oxen.

Yer Christmas be passed, then let horse be let blood,
For many a purpose it dooth them much good.

This operation was believed to increase their strength and staying power and to protect them from sickness in the coming year. Derbyshire farmers thought it most beneficial if

carried out during the waning of the moon. For three days afterwards the animals were allowed to rest.

Copies of 'The Horse's Prayer' hung in many farmhouses and were sometimes found nailed on the wall of a stable. It was often recited by children on Saint Stephen's day.

Up the hill, beat me not,
Down the hill, hurry me not,
On the plain, spare me not,
In my stall, forget me not.

December 28th is CHILDERMAS DAY which commemorates the 'Holy Innocents,' the young children slaughtered by King Herod.

It was thought to be the unluckiest day in the year and Derbyshire people would hesitate to embark on any new enterprise on this day, especially if babies under the age of two were concerned, for disastrous results might be expected. Children often gave each other a 'good hiding', playfully, because it was Childermas.

from

A Meet of the Meynell

THE REVD K.G. PACKARD

The Meynell country lies half and half in Derbyshire and Staffordshire. The landscape and country on the Derbyshire side are almost equal to the classic hunting country of Leicestershire. For generations the hunting days have been Monday and Thursday in Derbyshire and since George III's day the opening meet has been at Sudbury. Boxing Day meets have, until recently, always been held at Kedleston Hall. This extract is taken from Hunting Counties *by F.A. Stewart.*

Not long after Christmas 1930, there had been some doubt whether hounds would hunt at all, and a smaller field than usual met Mr Hilton Green and the bitch-pack on the broad green at Twyford crossroads. A few minutes past eleven found the company jogging up the lane past Stenson Lock to Hell Meadows. Here a fox at once jumped up but it was soon apparent that scent was poor. This, however, is a circumstance which has never been allowed to discourage Meynell followers in recent seasons, and soon horses were crashing down the muddy lane which borders the covert, and over the grasses by Bakeacre Lane, where the pack were running hard into the

A female 'heavy swell'

teeth of a nor'easter. The fox was headed at the Derby–Uttoxeter main road, but Mr Hilton Green's uncanny prescience of a fox's movements put hounds right at once and most followers never knew they had checked at all. Through the grounds of Pastures and alongside Mrs Kirkland's farmhouse they ran, and thence to the southern outskirts of Derby, to lose their fox in some complicated allotment gardens at Sunny Hill. Next came a fast twenty minutes with a fox from some kale of Mr Preston-Jones at Mickleover, straight to Burnaston and back to the big mental hospital, grass all the way. This fox literally escaped among the inmates of the asylum. Another short fast hunt followed from the Four Acres to Burnaston, the fox getting in near Etwall. Then came the turn of Radburne Rough. This renowned covert, always associated with the great squire of Radburne, the late Colonel R.W. Chandos-Pole, raises a feeling of tense expectancy whenever hounds draw there, so numerous have been the great runs from this covert. On the day in question there was silence for ten minutes, broken only by an occasional quiet cheer from

Away from Radbourne Rough looking towards Sutton, by Cecil Aldin

the huntsman. Then a hound threw her tongue, then another, then a third, soon there was music from the whole pack. It was plain that there were three or four lines, and when Frank Freeman, enjoying a busman's holiday from the Pytchley, halloaed a fox away, hounds were so divided that they did not get the best of starts. Still, they ran very nicely in a big right-handed ring by Lees Green, Haunted Hollow and under Radburne Hall to the Rough again. This time the fox did not linger and was viewed away by Jack Sturman, formerly huntsman of the Heythrop, to Dalbury Hollow. With a glorious cry the pack swept over the two brooks and through Captain Buckston's snug covert, Sutton Ash Gorse, in a beeline for three miles to cross the Hilton brook, below the well-known gorse, at the spot featured in Cecil Aldin's picture. Hounds flew on, bearing slightly right-handed, over the hill for Foston. Through the length of the top covert they went, and down by the old mill to Sapperton. Fresh foxes caused trouble here and after running a left-handed circle back to Foston, hounds were stopped at dusk. They had scored a 7-mile point in a little over two hours and hardly touched a ploughed field.

Christmas Letters from Edith Sitwell

Dame Edith Sitwell, DBE, D.Litt. (1887–1964) was the only daughter of Sir George Sitwell, Bt., of Renishaw Hall and sister of Sir Osbert and Sir Sacheverell Sitwell. She was one of the foremost and innovative poets of her generation. She is best known for Façade *– a series of poems set to music by Sir William Walton.*

To William Plomer

December 20, 1947 Renishaw Hall

My dear William,

This is just to wish you a very happy Christmas and New Year.

Personally, I loathe Christmas, in spite of being very greedy. But in the new year, one always hopes it can't be quite as bad as the previous one, although one's hopes are never realised.

I am so grateful to you, William, for having so kindly said you liked my 'Shadow of Cain', in *Horizon*. You are one of the only people who understand the poem. I send you, herewith, my two other Atomic Bomb poems. 'The Canticle of the Rose' was written after reading that vegetation is beginning to sprout at Hiroshima.

Edith Sitwell, left, as a young woman with her parents, Sir George and Lady Ida Sitwell, and brothers, Osbert and Sacheverell, from the painting by J.S. Sargent at Renishaw Hall

I went to London for two days, to see Osbert given the *Sunday Times* prize – but two days was quite enough for me. The luncheon party at the prize-giving was delightful, however. There was a man there who began talking to me by saying he knew you. I think I have got his name wrong, but it was either Frazer or Fleming, I think the latter. I thought at first, from his manner with her, that he was Lady Cunard's social secretary, but realised afterwards that she would scarcely have employed him in that capacity. He told me he was 'very amused' to see that you had put my 'Shadow of Cain' first on

your *Horizon* list. He ran no immediate risk in saying this, as we were both guests at a luncheon party given in honour of Osbert. He then, until I was at last released from him, expatiated on the other 'amusing' and 'surprising' choices.

I shall be coming up at Easter for about ten days, to look after Evelyn Wiel. I do hope you will be there, even if it is only for part of the time. I am proposing to have a giant luncheon party the Tuesday before Easter. But I'll write to you about that nearer the time.

Love, and all best Christmas wishes from Edith.

To Stephen Spender

14 December 1943 Renishaw Hall

Dear Stephen,

I was more than delighted and happy to receive the lovely 'Spiritual Exercises', some of which I am proud to have known before they reached their maturity – lovely then, and lovely now. They have an extraordinary perfection of sense and form. You have, really, a genius for producing a form and spirit that are one, – a form 'arising out of the properties of the material.' Nobody who was not a poet could guess that any *making* went to the poems. They seem to spring from you perfectly naturally like leaves from a bough, by a natural growth.

I find these poems start one on many different roads. Poetry ought to make one live, in one's own way, and these poems, like all your poems, make me live in my own way. Very few poets pack their lines with meaning as you do, and yet keep a universe of air round them. The lines are never breathless. Each meaning has its life of air. I hope I am explaining what I feel about them – which is much, and deep. I am *very* tired and despondent, and so find it difficult to express what I feel.

Realising that Christmas is upon us, and that you will therefore, probably, be unable to work at anything you want to, – I am sending you the poems I had been keeping back, so as not to interrupt you. *But you are not to read them until you feel inclined, and have nothing else to do.*

I sent you and Natasha, yesterday, my *Pleasures of Poetry*, which has *at last* turned up (a very old work). But it isn't my real Christmas card to you both.

That will be Sachie's new book, which I am expecting at any moment.* It *should* reach you before Xmas. I hope it will. It has some really gigantic things in it about the blitzes, – and one of the most extraordinary things about madness I have ever read. Also terrific things about beggars. It is a book of black sadness, but has a quality of greatness.

I hope you are not being driven mad by this wretched fireman's work. Really, looking at those poems, my blood boils as I think of it. . . .

Love to you and Natasha (to whom I am writing by the same post). 'They' now lose *all* letters, but I trust both will arrive. Edith.

And best wishes for Christmas. I hope you both gargle and take great care against the 'flu.

* *Splendours and Miseries*, published on 17 December.

Some Eyam Carols

CLARENCE DANIEL

Clarence Daniel was born in the plague village of Eyam where two members of his family died from the disease in 1666. He was an authority on Derbyshire local history and author of The History of Eyam; Pinnacles of Peak History; A Peakland Portfolio *and* Derbyshire Customs *from which the following extract has been adapted. He contributed many articles to local journals.*

The story of the Incarnation is a theme which has appealed more strongly to the imagination of minstrels than perhaps any other aspect of the life of Christ; just as it has inspired more artists to apply their gift to the portrayal of the Nativity than almost any other incident in Biblical history. Gifted poets have described their impressions of the first Christmas in language matched only by the enchanting settings of equally talented musicians. The mystic birth and being of the Babe of Bethlehem has inspired the sweetest music and most profound poetry of the Christian era.

Poets and musicians of lesser degree have joined in this spiritual pilgrimage to the stable shrine of Bethlehem to offer – like the Magi of old – gifts of golden words and perfumes of melody to the infant King. Some of these local compositions, it must be admitted, have little artistic merit. They are often stilted in conception, lacking in spontaneity, devoid of inspiration, and therefore unsuccessful in their appeal to popular imagination. Yet it is

Derbyshire carol singers including Mr Samuel Slack of Tideswell and Mr Chadwick of Hayfield

rather regrettable that few people attempt to write the words or music of carols today, not for commercial profit and with an eye on 'the charts', but with the same sincerity as the erstwhile producer of the home-spun carol which lives on in folk-song.

Many of the carols were equivalent in emotional quality, character and atmosphere to the negro spiritual. Their success depended upon rhythm rather than rhyme; upon musical

rather than metrical construction. Visually the words were often commonplace, and the carols depended upon harmony and musical design for their creative force and appeal. Sometimes they had a lively, lilting quality which mirrored the mood of the season, while others possessed a more tranquil movement and something of the same soothing quality as the German tune 'Stille nacht'.

The Oxford Book of Carols says: 'Carols are songs with a religious impulse that are simple, hilarious, popular and modern . . . Carol literature and music are rich in true folk-poetry and remain fresh and buoyant even when the subject is a grave one. But they vary a good deal: some are narrative, some dramatic, some personal, a few are secular; and there are some which do not possess all the typical characteristics.'

Referring to the dancing origin of the word 'carol', the Oxford Book says: 'The carol, in fact, by forsaking the timeless contemplative melodies of the Church, began the era of modern music, which throughout has been based upon the dance. But, none the less, joyfulness in the words has been sometimes discarded by those who were professionally afraid of gaiety.' The Oxford anthology contains a carol from Castleton which is of 17th century origin, and which begins by urging the need to remember the solemn character of Christmas:

All you that are to mirth inclined,
Consider well and bear in mind
What our good God for us hath done,
In sending His beloved Son.

But later carol-makers refused to have the mood of merriment repressed or their music muted by contemplation on the latter events in the life of the Patron of the festival. An Eyam draper, Mr J.T. Hancock, reflected something of this rebellion against restraint in one of his compositions.

Merry, merry Christmas everywhere,
Cheerily it ringeth through the air,
Christmas bells, Christmas trees,
Christmas odours on the breeze.
Why should we, so joyfully, sing with grateful mirth?
See! the Sun of Righteousness beams upon the earth.

Another carol, attributed to Richard Furness, the Eyam poet-schoolmaster, also suggests a feeling of exultation in both words and music:

We twine our festive garlands
  For the happy Christmas morn,
When bloomed the Rose of Sharon
  And the Holy One was born;
When tidings of Salvation
  Burst the Captive's prison bands,
When valleys were exalted
  And the mountains clapped their hands.

Furness, who was schoolmaster at Dore, was in the habit of composing the words and music of a carol every Christmas, and a footnote to his collected works says that he was responsible for over thirty such works. The fact that some of his carols are still sung in Peakland villages more than a century after his death, is some criterion of their poetical and musical worth.

Another Eyam musician, Mr George Dawson, is remembered each Christmas by a tune he composed to the familiar 'Hark! the herald angels sing'. He was a shoemaker by trade and the music came tumbling in a cascade of inspiration while busy at his work. Flinging down his tools, he snatched up a leather shoe sole and jotted down the notes until he had an opportunity to transfer them to more conventional writing material.

A Modern Tradition

ROBIN GIBBARD

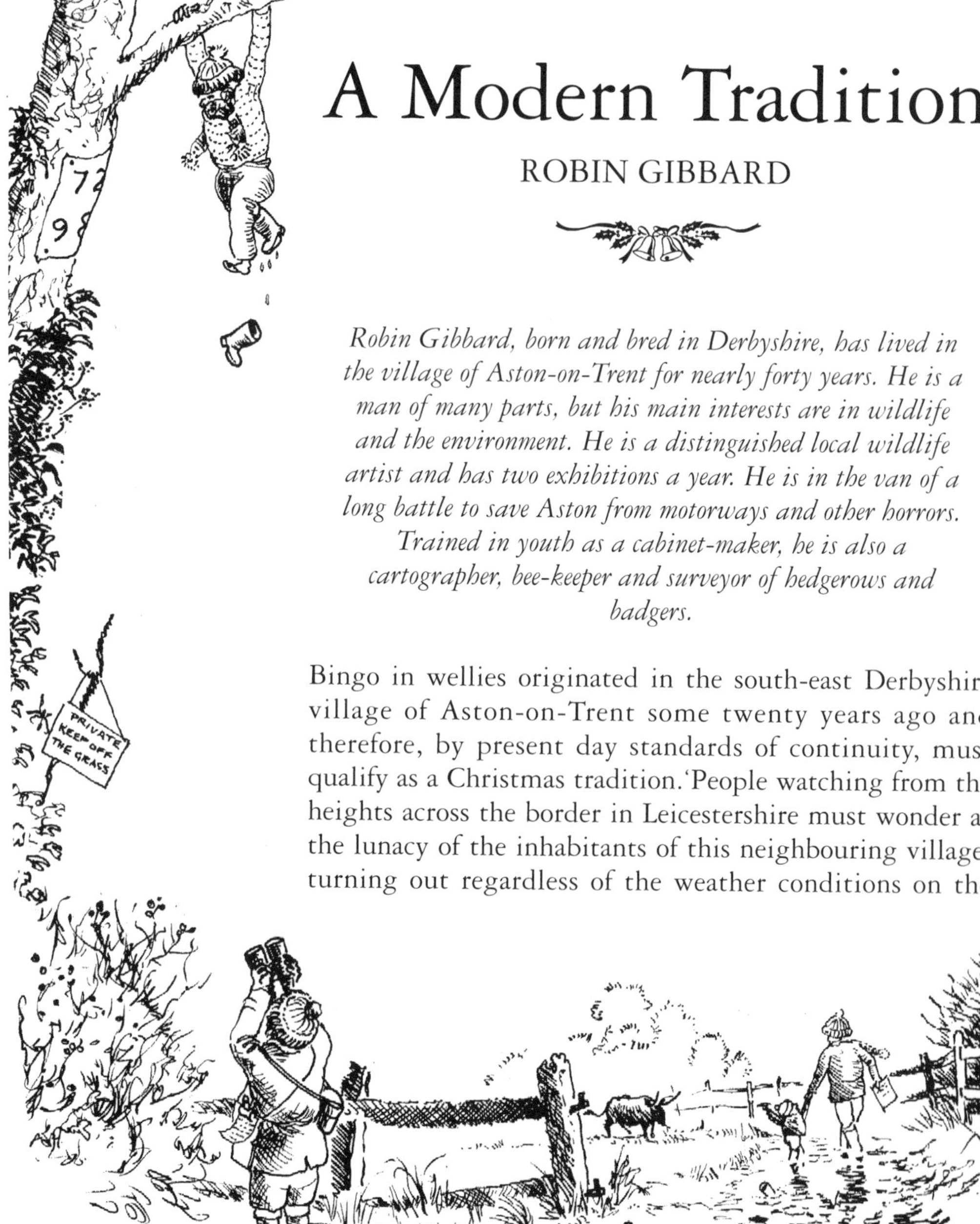

Robin Gibbard, born and bred in Derbyshire, has lived in the village of Aston-on-Trent for nearly forty years. He is a man of many parts, but his main interests are in wildlife and the environment. He is a distinguished local wildlife artist and has two exhibitions a year. He is in the van of a long battle to save Aston from motorways and other horrors. Trained in youth as a cabinet-maker, he is also a cartographer, bee-keeper and surveyor of hedgerows and badgers.

Bingo in wellies originated in the south-east Derbyshire village of Aston-on-Trent some twenty years ago and therefore, by present day standards of continuity, must qualify as a Christmas tradition.'People watching from the heights across the border in Leicestershire must wonder at the lunacy of the inhabitants of this neighbouring village, turning out regardless of the weather conditions on the

day after Boxing Day every year to plod across field and flood, snow and mud, to stop periodically and write things down on each others' backs and then disappear into the village hall to re-emerge an hour later, wobbling a little.

Perhaps it is time to explain these strange goings-on. In the dim and distant past of Aston's history one Mr Adams thought up and organised a small car treasure hunt (people could not afford large cars then) giving out cards with different sets of numbers on. This proved to be very popular socially, ending up as it did in a local hostelry. His son Ken later developed this idea and every mid-summer on a fine evening (all evenings were fine then) a continuous stream of slightly larger cars set forth to follow the clues typed out. Landmarks of various denominations were investigated in the search – Marstons, Home Ales, John Smiths etc. – until all the clues were unearthed and solved.

Then, not satisfied with inflicting this upon us, Ken Adams dreamed up the ultimate torture – walking! In the '70s walking was definitely old hat (by now cars had grown larger and the suspension much improved) nobody walked any more; legs had already started to wither. Imagine the consternation in the community when a public notice appeared, 'Walking off the Christmas Pud' – the village *will* assemble at the memorial hall at 10.30 to collect bingo cards and proceed via a designated route to collect numbers nailed to trees, posts etc. and return to said memorial hall for compulsory mince pies, 'laced' coffee and prizes if you're lucky.

We all approached this warily of course, as country bumpkins do (turning up in our Jags and Range Rovers). Smiling, almost jovial, Ken and Ann Adams met us and issued us with our bingo cards and a monologue to direct our feet to the first clue, several numbers surreptitiously displayed on a post. To mark our card, of course, we only had one pen and its owner was dragging behind talking to the only blonde to turn out

that day. It was a case of 'present backs' in those days to obtain a suitable firm writing surface. This problem overcome, and the next clue proceeded to via a few well chosen muddy gateways, it started to rain and in no time at all the bingo card was beginning to look frayed around the edges. Clue after clue, number card after number card followed, interspersed with field gates and stiles, flooded fields and lanes until finally, caked in good old Trent Valley mud, we stomped into our memorial hall. Ken was beaming; his wife Ann, horrified at the sight of us, administered first aid, in the form of rum coffee and mince pies. Had we won a prize? All the numbers had been duplicated and were hanging on the walls for a double check. Had we trudged for hours in appalling conditions for nothing? Our by now disintegrated bingo card, carefully restored by the youngest member of the family, revealed that we had won a prize.

For the next few years we came to expect this torture at Christmas and mid-summer until finally Ken's nerve broke and he relented, only retaining the post-Boxing Day event. Even this he relinquished some years ago, passing it on to the Aston Bellringers who now open the event to all comers.

The test of stamina – the constant bowing the head against the blizzard, writing with numbed fingers, holding a blunt stump of pencil on soggy paper on someone else's back, digesting the inevitable mince pies and forcing down large quantities of laced coffee is not without its compensations. The bell-ringers do allow us to pay for the privilege and say this helps to keep their bell-ropes in good order!

These days, modern times, routes have been known to be cancelled and bypassed as 'impassable with mud'. Clipboards are now almost compulsory and bingo cards are protected with polythene. The green wellington has been invented to blend with farmyard fallout and surmounts most of the hazards experienced. In fact progress dictates – after last year's

experience we are fitting our dogs with snorkelling gear. Some property owners even allow passage across private land for that one day to allow a variation of walk year by year. The mince pies have improved too (no more of Ken's leftovers) and the prizes have become more numerous as the number of participants increases, though I suspect certain individuals never leave the hall by the condition of their boots and the number of 'coffees' they have consumed. It is a great tradition!

Christmas at Chatsworth – Above Stairs

LADY ANNE HOLLAND-MARTIN

Lady Anne Holland-Martin, MBE, was the youngest daughter of the 9th Duke of Devonshire, Governor-General of Canada and Lord Lieutenant of Derbyshire, and sister of the 10th Duke and of Lady Dorothy Macmillan. She married, for the third time, Mr Victor Montagu who renounced his title as 10th Earl of Sandwich.

Lady Anne here recalls the vanished era of pre-war country houses in the days of armies of servants when great houses were lived in as was intended.

We all know that 'Christmas comes but once a year' and that is on December 25th, but how different Christmas and December 25th can be in different parts of the world. In the Antipodes no doubt the hot sun would be shining, in the northern stretches of the Soviet Union it would probably be grey, frozen, snowbound. In Derbyshire on December 25th and round about the Christmas Season, it is somewhere between the two – certainly not hot, but sometimes sunny, rather grey at times, often rather frosty and occasionally very snowy.

The Christmases which I am going to try to write about were those spent at Chatsworth in the 1920s and 1930s. During those years all members of the family that could possibly manage it would come to Chatsworth for Christmas, and because it was such a very large family there was not much room for other visitors. A few more distant relations and old friends came, and, because they always did so, Christmas would not have been complete without them.

Chatsworth – West Front

The party usually consisted of my mother and father, their two sons and their wives, five daughters and their husbands, grandchildren in increasing numbers until the total of twenty-two was reached, and about eight other relations and friends, together with my mother's secretary, who was greatly loved by all and without whom it is hard to imagine a Christmas at Chatsworth. Therefore the number living in the house, excluding the household servants and the nurses, nursery maids, maids and valets brought by visitors, numbered usually somewhere round about forty-five. In all well over ninety people would be sleeping in the house.

No doubt the entertaining and the festivities may not be considered to have been on a very grand scale by those who remember the pre-World War I days, but it must be almost as hard for the generation now growing up to imagine over ninety being in one house (other than an institution or hotel) and people coming to stay bringing with them a nannie and nurserymaid and perhaps a personal maid and valet, as it is for us to imagine life without motor cars and telephones.

At this stage it is perhaps interesting to consider for a moment what this horde of family and visitors meant for the household servants. At the best of times there must always be a great amount of work to be done in a large house if it is to be kept as it should be. At these Christmas parties the work was tremendous. As I have already said over ninety people would be living in the house. Excluding afternoon tea this would mean that 270 meals had to be cooked a day. There would be dining-room meals, probably schoolroom breakfast and supper for the children aged from about eight to twelve. Nursery meals for the little children, their nannies and nursery maids. Steward's Room meals for the upper servants, Servants' Hall meals for the others. Added to all this regular work, on the days when the men were shooting there would be the shooting lunches to be prepared, and for those

who were hunting, sandwiches to be cut. Besides the normal food to feed such a vast company there would be turkeys to be cooked, about 1,000 mince pies and 80 plum puddings made and 11 Christmas cakes baked. That is only to mention the work of one section of the household, but naturally each and everyone was affected. With all this work involved at Christmas parties, I never remember hearing a word of complaint or grumbling. Perhaps that was because the party chiefly consisted of children, or perhaps just because it was Christmas.

The party would usually collect between about December 19th to 23rd and though some would probably leave after New Year, most of the mothers and children would stay anyway for ten days to two weeks or, if they happened to live in London, even longer.

The question of the journey to Chatsworth for Christmas was one fraught with anxiety because of the excessively uncertain climatic conditions. If one motored, it was a help, as so much could be stuffed into a car and inevitably there was always a vast amount of luggage and parcels to be transported. Against that there would probably be a fog or the roads would be snowy or icy making the drive most unpleasant. The trains, which seemed the most sensible means of conveyance, had the disadvantage of being very crowded, would probably be late and, anxious mothers felt, would be bound to be full of tiresome other children all with colds and probably measles as well! It usually ended with children going with nurses by train, mothers going in cars with the luggage and parcels, and fathers and other visitors following at the last moment by trains which they hoped would be comparatively comfortable, the returning rush of schoolchildren already being safely home. Two particular journey incidents I remember. One, when a train which was thought to stop at Matlock failed to do so and a party of ten children and attendants were swept

on to Millers Dale; and another occasion when two of my brothers-in-law coming from London to Chesterfield found the road to Chatsworth blocked by snow and had to return to spend Christmas Eve in the Midland Hotel, Derby, finally reaching Chatsworth via Matlock on Christmas Day.

On Christmas Eve, the house would be decorated with holly and other evergreens and a huge Christmas tree would appear in the Painted Hall. It was an ideal setting and looked very beautiful when decorated and illuminated, especially in the days when only candles were used.

One evening before Christmas the choir from Edensor Church would come up to the house and sing carols in the Painted Hall.

After dinner on Christmas Eve was perhaps for the grown-up members of the party almost the best moment of all the

Christmas tree in Chatsworth's Painted Hall

Christmas festivities and one especially loved by my father. When the children had gone to bed and it was hoped they were asleep, their mothers would bring down to the drawing-room the stockings which had been hung up, and there fill them. It took a long time, because everyone wanted to look at what everyone else had got. Small mechanical toys were tried and quite often broken. False noses, funny hats, were tried on, tricks and puzzles were experimented with – it is doubtful if the children had more enjoyment opening the stockings on Christmas morning than the grandparents and parents had filling them on Christmas Eve. Eventually all would be filled and the stockings safely returned to the foot of each bed.

Christmas Day itself would start either by going to the Early Service at Edensor Church or by the opening of the stockings according to the age of the individual. Breakfast would follow and after breakfast and before Church there would be a great deal of present giving. Everyone from the age of about four upwards would go to Church and then there would be a slight pause before an enormous luncheon would be consumed. In the afternoon, the children would go out of doors and if it was snowing or frosty, which was often the case, there would be tobogganing or skating. Most of the older people would stay in to listen to the King's broadcast, and then go out of doors and take some form of exercise. Tea would be early with a lovely Christmas cake and afterwards the official Christmas Tree. Everyone in the house would come into the Painted Hall, the tree would be lit and my mother and father would give their presents. There would be something for each person, family, friends, household servants and visiting servants. It was all done very informally, and therefore was fun and friendly. My mother and father would give some presents themselves and others their small grandchildren would give for them, but with so many people there it took a long time to go through all the presents. After the tree, for

the little children the day would be nearly at an end, they would have their supper and go to bed. The children from seven upwards who normally had schoolroom supper would be allowed on Christmas night to stay up for dinner in the dining-room, and though by that time the very young ones perhaps did not want to eat much more, there were always lovely crackers, and fruit and sweets, and they felt very grown up. After dinner everyone would play games until, exhausted, replete and very happy, they eventually went to bed.

In writing about Christmas in a 'Great House' and that house being one's home, it is impossible to stop at Christmas Day, because so much of what was inevitably regarded as part of Christmas happened afterwards.

On Boxing Day there was always a Meet of the High Peak Harriers of which my eldest sister and brother-in-law were masters during many of these years. Hunting with the Harriers was a great event in which all the children who could ride (and some who couldn't very well) took part. Children who had ponies would bring them with them, others would hire them, but that was so to speak only the beginning of it. The Meet often being a long way away, it was impossible (this was before the days of numerous horse boxes) to get the smaller ponies there on the morning itself. This meant either riding or leading them to a convenient distance the day before, finding a kind farmer who would either allow his stable to be used or had a field for them to be turned out in for the night, and then starting out early the next morning to collect the pony and get it, its saddle, bridle and rider to the Meet. Strangely and luckily enough in all these years, though horsemanship was not always of the highest standard, I do not remember any child having a serious fall.

Another activity of Christmas was theatricals, which the children themselves started by organising. They always said they wished for no help (a polite way of saying interference),

from any grown up person and started off full of enterprise and enthusiasm. They usually blithely invited the entire household to attend, but about two days before the performance was due to be given, frantic appeals for help would come. There was difficulty over the costumes, the scenery, so and so couldn't remember his part, but all always went well on the day. The programme was most varied, ranging through Biblical scenes, tableaux, one-act plays, singing and dancing. What made it all much more fun for both performers and audience, was Chatsworth having a proper theatre with scenery, lights, trap doors in the floor, and so on, to act in. Performers whether good or bad were always most enthusiastically applauded.

The school treat was a regular yearly event of the Christmas holidays and was usually held during the second week of January. Children from Baslow, Beeley and Pilsley schools (there was no school at Edensor at this time), and their teachers and the Sunday School children and their teachers, would come.

The children would arrive in the middle of the afternoon and go straight to the theatre for an entertainment, usually a conjuror, then come down to the Orangery where at long tables they would have tea and crackers. After tea they would go into the Statue Gallery (the statues having been moved to one side) where the Christmas tree had been brought from the Painted Hall and have their presents. Each school had a table in different parts of the room and the presents would be given out by my mother and father and other members of the family. Every child's present had its name on it and a list was kept giving the age of the child and the presents of the previous year or two. When the presents had all been given the children would stand round the tree, the Edensor vicar would make a little speech calling for 'Three cheers for the Duke and Duchess,' everybody would sing 'Auld Lang Syne,' and then

Chatsworth from the south-east

the children would leave. As they said goodbye each child was given an orange, an apple and bag of sweets. It was a very happy afternoon.

Looking back over the years it seems to me that these Christmases which were certainly 'Christmas in a Great House' were even more 'Christmas at home.' The House was and is a great one, the entertaining, the festivities, the food, the fruit, the flowers were all on a fitting scale to the house, but there was nothing over-lavish, over-grand, smart for the sake of being smart. Because of the bigness of the house and the bigness of the family, it nowadays all seems rather tremendous and unreal. But at the time to those who were taking part, I think they felt that they were periods to be looked forward to with happy anticipation and excitement and certainly now to be remembered with immense gratitude and thankfulness as times of 'peace and goodwill'.

Christmas at Chatsworth – Below Stairs

HENRY BENNETT

Henry Bennett was a footman at Chatsworth in the 1930s. He married a local girl from the village of Ashford-in-the-Water and they are both buried there. He left Chatsworth to work for Lord Athlone and later became for some years page to HM the Queen. The Duchess of Devonshire described him as '. . . a really nice man with a marvellous sense of humour . . . when he was buried at Ashford the flowers from most members of the Royal Family were very beautiful indeed. They all loved him'. This account is taken from The House *by the Duchess of Devonshire.*

All the family came for Christmas, so it was always a large party. With so many grandchildren – twenty, I believe, at this time – it meant six nurseries with six nannies and six nursery-maids who were responsible for cooking breakfast, porridge and toast, but the Steward's Room footman was detailed to carry all the nursery food from the kitchen, which was certainly a difficult undertaking with such a large house party, as it meant a large number of people for meals. On Christmas Day

Henry Bennett in semi-state livery, 1928

quite a number of children came to the Dining-Room for lunch, some having to sit on cushions to reach the table.

The tall Christmas tree was gaily decorated in the Painted Hall, with a cheerful log fire burning in the fireplace. The presents were given out to the staff by Their Graces and members of their family. The footmen for several years received six pairs of black socks, which were useful and always meant you were suitably dressed with your livery and black shoes. One year I was given a black and white scarf.

Christmas tea was laid on round tables in the Gold Drawing-Room, and except for babies in arms, all came for tea; there was always a grand spread of Christmas cakes. One year the Hunting Tower was depicted and cakes in the shape of yule logs, all made by the different stillroom maids, and of course an abundance of crackers. Babies in arms, carried by their devoted nannies, arrived in time to see the tree light up. The outdoor activities meant some guests would be late for lunch, so hot food was left in the dishes and placed in the large steel fenders in front of the fires to keep hot – no heated trolleys in those days.

Henry Bennett and Chatsworth housemaids

If the House was only occupied with Their Graces and Miss Saunders we were allowed off duty every other day, from after lunch. We were lucky in being able to play golf; some played football and cricket in season, otherwise tennis. In the winter we always had snow, so we indulged in tobogganing. We enjoyed dances at the Institute, which it was then called, and visited the neighbouring villages for whist drives and dances. If we became bored we did numerous jigsaw puzzles, and we had quite a craze for making woollen rugs.

When we moved to Bolton Abbey or Hardwick there was no electric light; oil lamps and candles were the order. A man was kept to see that the lamps contained oil, wicks trimmed and lamp glasses cleaned. It was the footmen's duty to put the lamps around the house. His Grace invariably liked candles, so quite a number of lighted candles adorned his study. When the ladies had retired late at night, the footmen had to extinguish the lamps, and place electric torches, silver candlesticks and matches outside the Drawing-Room for the guests to pick up and light themselves to their rooms, the order being that the last gentleman to leave the Drawing-Room saw that all lamps left there were extinguished. It proved so popular, and allowed us to retire earlier, that this plan was adopted at Chatsworth.

I enjoyed my seven years' service at Chatsworth, and over the years have benefited from the knowledge and experience gained there.

Christmas in Kinder

PAM GEE

Mrs Pam Gee moved into the Kinder district to live in the village of Hayfield in 1959 with her husband who has long connections with the area. She loves the district and, although originally a city dweller, has adopted the place as her own. She is a retired schoolmistress and for a long time has been a regular contributor to her local newspaper The High Peak Recorder *and its predecessor* The Courier. *This extract is from her book* Kinder People.

Christmas on the Kinder farmsteads was very much a family affair but, of course, Christmas Day could never be a complete holiday. There were cows to milk, eggs to collect, cattle and sheep to feed and all the regular farm tasks to be done as usual.

The rooms were brightened with trails of ivy, branches of larch and home-made paper chains. Very little berried holly grew in the valley and no one would dream of buying any. Not many families had a Christmas tree though the children from Ashes Farm had a young fir cut by a servant from the wood above the house. It was decorated with candles and a few precious, fragile, glass blown baubles saved from year to year.

The Marriott children from Hill House also had permission to cut a tree. Wilfred, one of the older brothers, remembered how one year they all set out in the snow to cut their tree. It

was quite dark by the time they had it tied to the sledge, so with a lantern to light the way, they sang carols at the top of their voices to stop the little ones being scared on the haunted hillsides.

Thick, knitted stockings were hung from the knobs of brass bedsteads or tied to the four poster. At dawn they were pounced on by excited small children who had been awake half the night. The contents hardly varied: nuts, oranges, a glossy red apple, a tangerine in silver paper, barley sugar twists, a pink sugar mouse with a white cotton tail, a gold mesh net full of chocolate coins and a shiny new penny or threepenny bit in the toe.

If there were toys they were small hand made objects like a top, a monkey-on-a-stick or a catapult whittled by someone in a spare moment. Everyone vividly remembered the delightfully guilty feelings of eating chocolate in bed before breakfast, half expecting a scolding.

Girls had been busy for weeks making presents for their parents and relatives, working in secret to produce bookmarks, needlecases, penwipers, embroidered texts or handkerchiefs hemmed with the neatest of stitches.

Thrifty farmers gave their children something plain and practical to wear. Wives did a great deal of knitting in the evening lamplight, for lost mittens and scarves were usually replaced as presents and socks, hats and jerseys were always wearing out.

Small girls, as ever, longed for a doll, but their wishes were not put first in a household where every penny was hard earned. One daughter had to wait until the January sale so that father could buy it at a reduced price! She lived in an agony of suspense in case the lovely doll was sold to some luckier child. Somehow by the time she held it in her arms, a lot of the thrill had gone, as the pink lace dress was shop-soiled and dusty. Another girl who had begged for a baby doll in a long, white robe, found that

she was expected to share it with her three sisters! A third child gazed at a fairy doll in a village shop for weeks. It had gauze wings, a silver wand and was dressed in a frilly, white net skirt. In her stocking she found a rag doll made from recognisable scraps of cast off dresses! Though she loved it, the bitter disappointment she felt at the time is still a strong memory.

A young boy hoping for a book of the latest adventure stories, got a Sunday collection of improving texts and cautionary tales. Another had to put all the fruit and nuts back on the dish to be eaten when mother gave permission. The saddest story was told by a lady in her eighties. Tears filled her eyes as she remembered how she had seriously displeased her step-mother by creeping into the parlour to play with her doll on the Sabbath. It was snatched from her arms and its beautiful china face smashed against the wall 'to teach her a lesson'

At Stones House Farm, Muriel never wanted a doll. She hung a rope and a strap on the bottom of her bed and Father Christmas always put her new calf in the bottom shippon!

Very little extra was bought in for the special day except a large pork pie for tea. Huge joints of home-cured pork and ham with all the trimmings followed by a round plum pudding boiled for hours in a white cloth, left no one hungry. All the children hoped to find a silver charm in their slice of pudding but no girl wanted to get the silver thimble for this meant she would die an old maid!

The postman delivering mail on Christmas morning was warmly welcomed at every house with a large glass of whisky, hot elderberry wine or mulled ale spicy with nutmeg. If he was lucky, Annie Marriott might offer a mince pie with her special mincemeat in it containing the secret ingredient of a little chopped liver!

Although times were often hard there was never any shortage of fuel. Most farms had their own small wood nearby

'The postman delivering mail on Christmas morning was warmly welcomed ...'

which was in constant use. One man, too lazy to cut up his yule log, propped it on a stool in front of the fire and pushed it with his foot as it burned! Unfortunately few ever replaced what was cut and young seedling trees rarely survived the attention of sheep and rabbits.

The history of the Kinder forests being used by local people goes back to the days of 1285 when it was recorded that 'The King's wood of Kynder' had been injured to the value of 16 shillings by the villagers and that 300 oaks had been converted into pales.

People once had the right to cut free turf on the moor for their fires. Local benefactor, Joseph Hague, left 40 acres on Leygate Moor to the poor people of Hayfield 'for ever,' in a will dating from 1781. Up to 1922, Ishmael Pursglove from Hayfield, fearless and determined, defended this privilege and

Kinder area from Lantern Pike looking over the hamlet of Little Mayfield to the edge of Kinder Scout plateau

used to lead a procession once a year carrying sacks and a specially shaped turf-cutting spade along the wide cart road behind Didsbury Terrace. 'He was a lone voice crying in the wilderness'. No one in the Parish Council thought the Turfury Rights worth preserving except Mr James Garside, and his idea that the National Trust be involved was not accepted. The area became enclosed with other land on the moor and the cart road was walled off. In 1969 the rights were again investigated and an attempt was made to get them back but the Turfery now marked on maps as 'Poor Man's Piece' or 'Old Pits Plantation' is totally lost to the people of Hayfield and Kinder.

Christmas on the farmsteads was a time for friends and relations to visit each other's houses, to talk, sing, admire the latest baby and to enjoy the plentiful food and drink. It was the last opportunity to relax before the hardest part of the winter with its dark days of snow and ice.

Christmas Customs

CLARENCE DANIEL

Peaklanders of the past have always acknowledged the coronation of Christmas as the most important event in the calendar of the Church, even though many of them have favoured feasting rather than fasting, and laid emphasis on the secular rather than the sacred character of the festival. At every level of society it has been recognised as an occasion for music, mirth and merriment; for gaiety, greetings and goodwill. It

gave opportunity for the rich man in his castle to remember the poor man at his gate, and provided an oasis of light in the desert of dark and dreary days of winter. As far back as the 17th century, Philip Kinder wrote of Peaklanders:– 'They love their cards. The miners at Christmas tyme will carry tenn or twenty pounds about them, game freely, returne home againe, all the year after good husbands.' But there have also been those of studious mind and serious disposition who 'rejoiced with exceeding great joy' along with the Wise Men, patiently watching with the shepherds by their camp-fires and listening with rapture to the angelic melodies of heaven. And as a result of their meditation upon the eternal mysteries of the Incarnation, they have bequeathed to posterity a wealth of carol literature and music.

At Renishaw Hall, home of the Sitwells, preparations for Christmas began early in November with the brewing of a couple of hogsheads of Christmas beer, and the making of a 'brawne' – valued at £2 – which was equivalent in price to four muttons and forty turkeys.

Turning from the magnificent meals served in the mansions, to the homelier fare of the cottages, we find that Christmas was celebrated on a much less lavish scale, yet with the same spirit of hospitality and goodwill. The season began with the drinking of a posset. This was primarily a Christmas beverage, although its beneficial properties made it a popular drink for winter evenings. It was a protection against chills and helped to induce sleep in those troubled with insomnia. The ingredients of posset included boiled milk or cream, ale, eggs, treacle, ginger, nutmeg and other spices. Posset was drunk on Christmas Eve, and specially designed pots were used for this family communion. Like the loving-cups they had handles on both sides to facilitate passing from one person to another. Sometimes the pots were ornamented with floral designs and often inscribed with the names of the owners.

A posset pot. Try turning it upside-down!

When the Christmas posset was served in homes where there were unattached sons and daughters, a silver coin and ring were placed in the pot, and each person took a spoonful in turn. The recovery of the ring was supposed to augur well for an early and happy marriage, while the one fortunate enough to scoop up the coin was assured of a prosperous future.

Incidentally, posset was one of the medicines used during the Eyam Plague, and a story is told of one patient who, having narrowly escaped premature burial by Marshall Howe, the self-appointed undertaker and sexton, recovered after drinking a posset.

At Bradwell the posset-drinking ceremony was illuminated by the burning of yule-logs and a special Christmas candle supplied by the village grocer to each of his customers. The

family also had a yule loaf which consisted of a round loaf on top of a four-pound loaf, both baked together, and sometimes surmounted with a figure. The first two customs no doubt had some significance with the pagan festival of rejoicing at the victory of light over darkness at the turn of the winter solstice.

Christmas Eve was also recognised in some villages as 'mischief night' when a certain amount of liberty was claimed for roguery and pranks played by village youths under cover of darkness. Gates were removed from their hinges; doors were securely fastened from the outside; water-butts were overturned; carts dispossessed of their wheels; sods dropped down convenient chimneys, and many other wilful acts were committed. Householders were equally alert, however, and sometimes the mischief makers were caught and chastised by angry victims.

Christmas was an occasion when distributions were made under the terms of charitable bequests, and the poor received gifts of food or footwear, clothing or coal, or sums of money. Under the conditions of the 17th-century will of Thomas Large, the Mayor of Chesterfield was directed to provide a convenient house for three poor persons who each received an annuity of £5 together with the gift of a blue cloth gown at Christmas. In the same town, inmates of the almshouses provided by Sarah Rose were furnished with a Christmas present of new gowns with the initials 'S.R.' worked on the right sleeves. Occupants of the St John's Hospital at Bakewell must have been proud as peacocks (crest of their patron) as they walked to church in their new Christmas gowns, each with a yellow and blue cross embroidered on the left breast, and with the instruction that these were to be worn at all times except when the owners were working. And there must have been envious glances cast at the inmates of Wilmot's almshouses at Derby who not only received new black gowns faced with red,

but a share in thirty yards of linen cloth for the making of shirts and smocks, and, to keep them warm within, a Christmas dinner. Furthermore, for good measure, they were the recipients of a new red cap each alternate year. Then at Melbourne, Henry Greene directed that four green waistcoats lined with green galloon lace should be given to four poor women on or before the 21st December. Thomas Gray went a step further, for he provided six waistcoats of grey cloth to be faced with baize or 'some other blue stuff' for the poor widows of Castle Donington and Melbourne.

Christmas at Melbourne

Christmas at Mountain Cottage

D.H. LAWRENCE

D.H. Lawrence was born in Eastwood on the Nottinghamshire–Derbyshire borders – 'the country of my heart' – in 1885 and died of tuberculosis at Vence in the south of France in 1930. The son of a miner, he was to become one of England's great literary figures, producing novels, short stories, essays, poetry and, not least, a prolific outpouring of letters which mirror all facets of his strange, vehement, tormented life.

These three letters were written when he and his German wife, Frieda, were living in Mountain Cottage (which looks just the same today) on a bend of the road which winds down steeply from the top of Middleton-by-Wirksworth to the Via Gellia far below. They were there for a year, from May 1918. It was a low-ebb time for Lawrence: work wasn't going well and they had very little money. The following winter was a terrible one in Derbyshire. The weather was ferocious and the dreadful post-war 'flu epidemic, which killed so many people, was raging in the district and they were both very ill. His depression comes through in the letters, but at least Christmas Day was happy – with no apparent food shortages!

A Derbyshire Christmas

Mountain Cottage
Middleton-by-Wirksworth, Derby.
20 Dec., 1918.

To Katherine Mansfield.

My Dear Katherine, –

So it is practically Christmas, and the shortest day. I wish you were better, so that we could kick off with a bit of a spree.

It snowed yesterday, and the dark valley was white. But it melted. To-day there is a powder of snow, and a slow sunshine. In the wild storm yesterday evening arrived my sister and her husband. They went again this morning at 7.0, and I watched them in the dark, slightly snowy greyness. We are going to Ripley on Christmas Day, after all – leaving here about 10.0. Think of us *en voyage*. They are having a turkey.

We went to Matlock yesterday, and got you this bit of the Derbyshire underworld. It is Fluor Spar – mined just near, and cut in Matlock. It is very difficult to cut. There is a purple sort – the common name for this stone is Blue John – but it was too expensive to buy you a purple bowl. And I like this yellow one. It is a golden underworld, with rivers and clearings – do you see it? For some reason, it is like Derbyshire.

I have a sort of feeling that you are not very well. But tomorrow is the *shortest* day, and then the tide turns. I do so want to do nice gay happy things, to start at once. I hate work, and I don't want to work – write, that is. I wish we'd had our Rananim – or got it. I should so love gaily and easily to mess about. I can't bear any feeling of any sort of *importance* in things any more. One wants to be nice and easy and insouciant.

The barber cut my hair and shaved me bald and made me look like a convict, clipping my beard; also gave me an ensuing cold – *Courage, mon ami, le diable vit encore.*

I'm supposed to be doing that little *European History*, and earning my living, but I hate it like poison, and have struck. Why work?

I hope you won't get this days and days before Christmas. Oh, did you send Pinker the stories? I've had no acknowledgement from him. And —— —— the Jung?

Greet Jack from me.

Many Christmas greetings – let's be born ourselves. Jesus is a back number – time our star riz.

D.H.L.

Mountain Cottage,
Middleton-by-Wirksworth, Derby.
22nd December, 1918.

To Lady Cynthia Asquith.

I don't know where you are spending Christmas – but hope you will have a high and festive time, and that Michael will suitably enjoy himself. We are going across to my sister's on Christmas Day, if ever I get so far – having got a bad cold, under which I crawl dismally for the time being. The weather is very dark and nasty, and Christmas is an institution that really should be abolished. I don't want to hear of it, it wearies me – I suppose you will be in town, tripping round and refusing turkey. But one needs the spring to come, when the skies will lift a bit and one can wander forth. Sorry the play irritated you. Keep it as long as you feel any use in keeping it. I wrote four nice little essays for *The Times*, nicely curried. *The Times* refrains from even acknowledging their receipt. I chuckle a little to myself, when my cold leaves me enough energy. Ah, what a happy day it will be, when I need not write any more – except a letter occasionally. I am tired of writing. We heard from F.'s mother in Baden-Baden. I believe

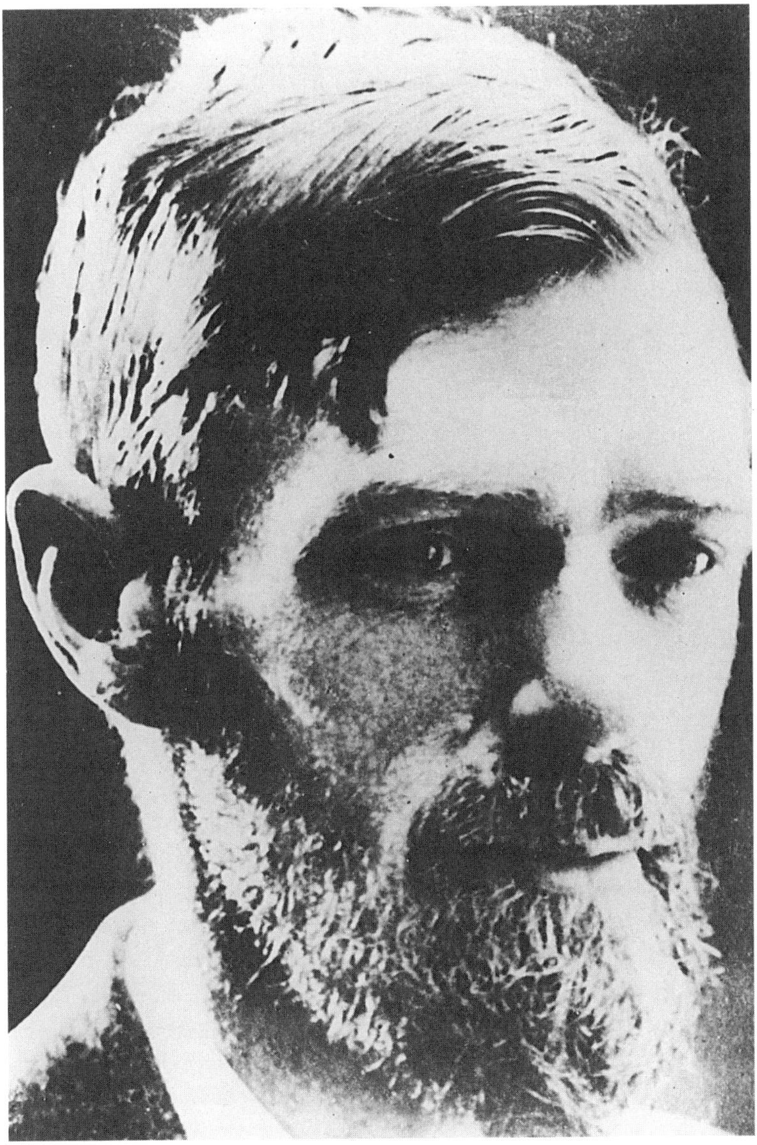

D.H. Lawrence

her godfather – Frieda's – has left her a legacy – he should have done: he has just died. I suppose the Allies will swallow it: just the thing that would happen to us. But then my brother-in-law is now Minister of Finance for Bavaria, so he might hook out the fish for us. Oh, my dear, —— —— if I had even £100 a year I would never write another stroke for the public. Pray that I may get this provision.

I don't know that my wishes for a festive Christmas are worth much, but here they are. F. sends also.

D.H.L.

c/o Mrs Clarke, Grosvenor Rd.,
Ripley, Nr. Derby.
Friday, 27 Dec., 1918.

To Katherine Mansfield.

My Dear Katherine, –

We got your parcel on Christmas morning. We had started off, and were on the brow of the hill, when the postman loomed round the corner, over the snow. It was all white and snowy and sunny, with a wind like an axe. I floated out my hanky for a flag over the snow, and Frieda dropped the tangerines in her anxiety to get the wheatsheaf unwrapped, and it was terribly cold and windy just on that edge. Frieda's wheatsheaf looked so strange, such a queer indescribable darkish colour, somehow elephant, over the snow which is so candid in comparison. It was queer and like Africa, and a bit like a meteor. She has worn it on her yellow slip, with the red silk shirt and red coat, at our two parties here – but I can't get used to it now, it seems like a little torch or brand of elephant-grey, tropical, lush twilight. Funny how things disturb one. But my hanky fluttered very nice and lively. I wish you could have been there on the hill summit – the valley all

white and hairy with trees below us, and grey with rocks – and just round us on our side the grey stone fences drawn in a network over the snow, all very clear in the sun. We ate the sweets, and slithered downhill, very steep and tottering. The children had the tangerines and the fan.

We read your letter in the wind, dropping down to Cromford. It made me feel weary, that we couldn't be all there, with rucksacks – I'd got mine on – setting off for somewhere good, over the snow. It *is* disappointing. And unless one decorates one's house for oneself alone, best leave it bare, for other people are all wall-eyed. I do so want to GET OUT – out of England – really, out of Europe. And I *will* get out. We must do it.

There was hardly any snow in the valley – all green, with the yew-berries still sprinkling the causeway. At Ambergate my sister had sent a motor-car for us – so we were at Ripley in time for turkey and Christmas pudding. My God, what masses of food here, turkey, large tongues, long wall of roast loin of pork, pork-pies, sausages, mince-pies, dark cakes covered with almonds, cheese-cakes, lemon-tarts, jellies, endless masses of food, with whisky, gin, port wine, burgundy, muscatel. It seems incredible. We played charades – the old people of 67 playing away harder than the young ones – and lit the Christmas tree, and drank healths, and sang, and roared – Lord above. If only one hadn't all the while a sense that next week would be the same dreariness as before. What a good party we might have had, had we felt really free of the world.

We had a second turn-to yesterday – and at half past eleven went roaring off in the dark wind to Dr Feroze's – he is a Parsee – and drank two more bottles of muscatel, and danced in his big empty room till we were staggered, and quite dazed. To-night we are going back to Middleton – and I feel infuriated to think of the months ahead, when one waits paralysed for some sort of release. I feel caged, somehow – and

I *cannot* find out how to earn enough to keep us – and it maddens me.

Still, it might be very much worse. One might be tied tight to a job, or to a sickness. I do wish you were better. But you *sound* stronger. I long to make *plans* – new plans. But not Europe: oh, God!

I pledge you 'the days to come'.

D.H.L.

Winter, Christmas and Children

RICHARD WRAGG

Richard Wragg, who compiled this anthology of children's Christmas poems, belonged to a family long-rooted in Derbyshire. His brother, Tom Wragg, was for many years first assistant Librarian and Keeper of the Collections at Chatsworth, under the legendary Francis Thompson, and later became Librarian and Keeper of the Collections himself. Richard Wragg wrote many articles on local Derbyshire topics.

Childhood has no time for spilt milk. Enjoyment of the present and mouth-watering anticipation of the future are part of the wonder of the time. Always the next adventure is bound

to be the most exciting and the best yet. So the child's year advances from one high point to another. After the freedom and holiday, long pleasures of summer days in the sun, come the fall of the year and dark winter. But the child is not dismayed.

There's ice on the duck pond,
There's frost in the lane
And the five-bar gate is frozen up again.

There's snow on the hillside,
There's drifts on the plain
And the five-bar gate is frozen up again.

But there's a light in the window,
Firelight flickers on the pane,
I'll jump the gate if it's frozen
And I'll soon be home again.

All the obvious enjoyment of the hardness of the season is there with the comfort and security of home. In winter, too, there are the trembling pleasures of being out in the dark.

The stars were shining,
But no moon, no cars
The night was cold
I trembled
I looked round,
I thought, 'Is there anybody behind that tree?'

I walked on looking back
But still no one in sight
I walked and walked
And walked

I saw a light,
A street light I knew, I was home at last.

However morning comes with the calm of a new day and the sameness of the usual daily routine.

A robin sings high in a tree
To tell us that he is at home.
The cats sit by the kitchen door
Waiting to come in.
Now I hear the milkman
Clashing crates and bottles of milk,
There's mother telling me breakfast is ready
Counting each step downstairs I go
To breakfast, goodbye and a new day at school.

Then ahead, beyond the fires of November, stands the glowing beacon of Christmas.

I got up and looked at my presents.
I was very excited,
I was dancing round the Christmas tree.
We had a lot of Christmas cards
Hanging on a piece of string above the fire.
We took the balloons off the ceiling
And played with them.
Soon dinner time came.
We had chicken.
Then we had Christmas pudding and custard.
After dinner we played games.
Soon we had tea.
We had sandwiches for tea
Then we had trifle.

After tea we were playing games again,
Snakes and ladders and blind man's buff.

But soon the child senses that Christmas is not all presents and parties and food and games.

On Christmas Eve a baby was born
It was God's son.
And the Shepherds came
And the Wise Men came
To Bethlehem
And they brought their gifts.
And the sheep stared at the baby
And the cow stared at the baby
All the animals stared at the baby
And all the people stared at the baby.

Yet the sights and sounds of the happy time can bring other thoughts.

As I was putting the holly over the fireplace,
I heard the bells ring for Christmas.
I was so happy Christmas was here
I thought of baby Jesus
Born in Bethlehem
With Mary his mother at his side.
The baby was laughing
I could hear him in my own mind
And I thought of little boys and girls
With no homes, no food to eat
And no beds to sleep on.

A similar concern can be for the whole world of Nature without the heartening warmth of the Christmas fire.

Once a year Christmas comes
Bringing happiness and cheer.
But to some animals
Joy and happiness don't come.
The disturbed dormouse is dead.
Birds are hungry and cold.
Outside the snow falls
Birds look for food
The hedgehog, long asleep,
Dreads waking too soon
For he might die.
But in the house the fire is warm
And chestnuts are cracking
While father and mother
Listen to the children's carols
And everyone is merry
But the animals.

With Christmas gone, over the hill of winter remaining stands the freshness of the new year and the friendly sun ever nearer, ever warmer,

The sun is a ball glittering
With sunshine in my eyes
When I look high, high in the sky
I cannot bear to look.
Out I go to play in the sun
The sun is warm, it makes me joy.
I look again, still the sun shines
The sun in the sky a ball glittering.

for the child knows that Spring will soon come with its pleasures and promise of the summer to follow.

Many flowers grow in our garden
Tulips, daffodils and crocus
Snowdrops and all the flowers of Spring.
I like to smell their many scents
And watch their glowing colours,
Red for the proud tulip
Yellow for the swaying daffodil
Purple for the little soldier crocus
White for the gentle snowdrop
All fighting in Spring's army
Waving their banners.

[Note: All the extracts are from the writings of children in a rural primary school in the county.]

Christmas Eve in a Derbyshire Village

THOMAS RATCLIFFE

Thomas Ratcliffe was born at Coxbench in 1843, the son of a stonemason. The following is an extract from his manuscript notes on mummers, plays, rhymes and folklore of Derbyshire and Nottinghamshire.

The old customs and amusements of Christmas time are dying out, and it is only here and there, in some out-of-the-way

spot, that the old ways still exist in all their rough simplicity. The present day is too polished for the old ways, hence they are dying out; some of them are quite dead, and it is only round some old-fashioned ingle-nook that the Christmas customs of a hundred years ago are kept up.

My memory takes me back thirty years, and some of the customs then common at Christmas in and about my childhood home are remembered with pleasure. The memory of them is all that remains, for here new ways are known, ways which do not seem in keeping with this festive season.

Christmas time really began on St Thomas's day, when all the old people, and not a few young ones, started out early in the morning and collected a 'Thomassing' from their better off neighbours, receiving the gifts of milk, cheese, creed wheat (for frumenty), oatmeal, flour, potatoes, mince pies, pig-puddings, and pork pies as a matter of course, and many a one got in this way quite sufficient with which to make merry on Christmas Eve, when in every cottage and house the festive board was spread as well as the means of the house would allow. Here were ale, pipes and tobacco, oranges, apples, and other fruits; sweets there were, including the famous home-made black-ball – a compound of treacle, sugar, butter, and ginger, boiled to a thick syrup, which hardened on cooling – a bottle of spirits, and home-made wine.

Lighting up every corner of the house with its cheerful blaze, and sending forth a delightful heat, the yule-log burned in the fireplace set alight by what was left of the last year's yule-log. The good-men of the house sat on the right of the fire, and the house-wife attended to the wants of all the family, who mostly contrived to gather at this time under the old roof. Generally the firelight was supplemented by several Christmas candles, and by this combined light games were played in part of the room cleared of furniture.

In that part of Derbyshire where I lived, bands of

Coming home for Christmas dinner at King's Newton

'mummers' or 'guisers', morris-dancers, waits, and carol singers, began house to house visits as soon as it was dark, and in no case were the 'guisers' denied admittance. They performed their play of 'St George' on the sanded open portion of the house floor, collected copper coins, and went to another place. The singers after one or two tunes outside, were asked in, and bread and cheese and spiced hot ale was served out to them, after which they sang 'Angels from the realms of glory', and departed.

Soon after ten o'clock a big bowl of ale posset was made, and this was served out to all in basins, and eaten with a spoon. This brew, which bore also the name of 'poor man's punch' was made of finely shredded bread, milk (boiling hot), hotted ale (not boiled), and nutmeg, ginger, and sugar, which were all mixed together, and a bottle of home-made wine

added. The rest of the evening was spent in supping hot spiced ale or elder wine and storytelling till midnight when the door was thrown open so that all could hear the singers without, singing 'Christians, Awake'. This over the visitors went home, and the family to bed.

Guising and Mumming in Derbyshire

S.O. ADDY

Sidney Oldall Addy was born in Sheffield in 1848 and practised there as a solicitor, dying in 1933. The following is an article which was published in the Derbyshire Archaeological and National History Society Journal *in 1907.*

I – THE OLD TUP

George Potter, of Castleton, told me in 1901 that when he was a boy the Christmas guisers in that village were about twenty in number. They wore masks, big hats, and short trousers.

At the present time a boy gets into a sack, the top of which is tied in such a way as to represent two ears or horns, or else

Guisers at Castleton at the turn of the century

the sack is surmounted by a real sheep's head. A second boy represents a butcher, and carries a knife in his hand; a third is dressed like a woman; a fourth, who has his face blackened, represents an old man, and carries a bowl or basin in his hand. They go from house to house singing.

As the singing goes on the butcher pretends to stick the tup, and the old man with the bowl or basin pretends to catch his blood. When the performance is ended they ask for a copper or two, and then they sing 'Christians, Awake.'

In 1867 Mr Jewitt printed a version of 'The Derby Ram.' It begins:

As I was going to Derby, sir,
All on a market day,
I met the finest ram, sir,
That ever was fed on hay.

The long version printed by Mr Jewitt tells us that the butcher who killed the ram was drowned in the blood, and that the boy who 'held the pail' was carried away in the flood. The maids in Derby begged for his horns; the boys begged for his eyes. As regards the skin we are told that –

The tanner that tanned his hide, sir,
Would never be poor any more,
For when he had tanned and retched it,
It covered all Sinfin Moor.

His jaws 'were sold to a Methodist parson for a pulpit to preach in'. In a note Jewitt tells us that another version of the ballad ends with the lines:

And if you go to Derby, sir,
You may eat a bit of the pie.

We may compare the Castleton version with one or two others. At Handsworth Woodhouse (in Yorkshire), near Sheffield, a real sheep's head is put on the top of the sack, and the boy inside the sack walks on his hands and legs so as to look like a sheep. The butcher pretends to kill the tup, and his servant holds a basin to catch the blood, as at Castleton.

That the ceremony of 'the old tup' was intended to confer a benefit on the people may be inferred from the practice of sweeping the house, which ... forms part of the guising at Handsworth Woodhouse. It is well known to anthropologists that this sweeping was intended to expel evil from the house.

The 'Old Tup'

At Eyam, in Derbyshire, women sweep their door steps on the first of March, and they say that unless you do this you will have fleas all the year.

II – THE OLD HORSE

At various places in North Derbyshire, such as Norton, Eckington, and Dronfield, a number of men used to go round with 'the old horse' on Christmas Eve. The body of the man who represented the horse was covered with cloth or tarpaulin, and the horse's head was made of wood, the mouth being opened by strings in the inside. When the men reached the door of a house, the man representing the horse got under the tarpaulin, and they began to sing.

Then follows a prose conversation amongst the mummers,

which is not worth preserving, because it has been so modernised as to have lost all its interest. The end of it is that the horse gets a new lease of life, and attempts to worry a blacksmith, who is called upon to shoe him. The play is ended by the following stanza:

The man that shod this horse, sir,
  That was no use at all,
He likened to worry the blacksmith,
  His hammer and nails and all.
    Poor old, etc.

I have been told by an old man in Eckington, now dead, and by another man in Sheffield, that formerly the mummers used to find out where an old horse was buried, and dig its head up.

It will be noticed that in North Derbyshire the horse is described as 'the *old* horse'. 'Throughout Yorkshire,' says Mr Henderson, 'the Christmas mummers carry with them an image of a *white* horse.' In Lancashire 'the old horse' was descibed as 'Old Ball'. and the ceremony was performed not at Christmas, but at Easter. It is said that 'Old Ball' is a favourite name for a cart-horse in Lancashire, and Dr Murray, in *The New English Dictionary*, conjectures that *ball* means a white-faced horse. He refers to Fitzherbert's *Husbandry*, 1523, which mentions 'a white rase or ball in the forehead'. I have never seen 'an image of a white horse' in Yorkshire myself. At Little Hucklow one of the guisers came to the door and said, 'Please will you see Ball?'

It seems as if the old horse, or white horse, was intended to personify the aged and dying year. The year, like a worn-out horse, has become old and decrepit, and just as it ends the old horse dies. But he rises again with the new year. The time at which the ceremony is performed, and its repetition from one

house to another, indicate that it was a piece of magic intended to bring welfare to the people in the coming year.

That ceremonies like 'the old tup' or 'the old horse' were of a magical nature may be inferred from the fact that they were sternly prohibited by Christian law-givers and moralists. Theodore, Archbishop of Canterbury, in his *Penitential*, forbade the practice of going about at Christmas dressed up like a young stag or an old woman, clad in the skins of animals, or wearing beasts' heads, and he declared that those who changed themselves into the forms of animals were to do penance for three years, because the thing was devilish.

Such heathenish practices were not confined to England, and in the fourth century we find St Augustine denouncing them in a sermon.

Christmas 'Cheer' 1878

The following is a report from a Derbyshire newspaper. The journalist who wrote this catalogue of misery must have been a fellow of melancholy disposition. *He is at it again after the festivities on page 124.*

The year which is drawing to a close will long be remembered as a most calamitous one. It began in anxiety and gloom, and it is ending in anxiety, and for many people, alas! misery and destitution. Happily, this country was not involved in hostilities with Russia, on account of the Eastern Question, though

that knotty problem has left us legacies of the Protectorate of Asia Minor, and the Afghan war. But though not directly engaged in the war between Muscovites and Moslems, the awful slaughter and the horrors that cannot be named, which marked its course, will cause 1878 to be set apart in the memory, as an altogether exceptional year. Exceptional, too, it has been in other respects. The Kaffir war, in our distant dependency of South Africa, shows no signs of coming to a conclusion; but, on the contrary, there are many indications that it will extend to another and more powerful race. CETEWAYO, the Zulu king, imagines that he has cause for dissatisfaction with the British authorities, and as he can muster some sixty thousand tolerably well-armed and well-drilled soldiers, there is cause for grave anxiety in the fact that only an insignificant force of British troops is opposed to him. Our countrymen out there are a mere handful when compared with the native races, and anything like a combination among them would but too probably terminate in disaster for us. But not for these things only will 1878 be remembered. It will be recalled as a year of commercial disaster. The bank failures have been numerous, that of the Glasgow Bank being peculiarly disastrous in its consequences, while their general effect has been such a shock to credit as to intensify the already existing depression in trade. Strikes and lock-outs must be credited with having contributed to still further increase the stock of individual suffering which has at length assumed most serious proportions. So serious, indeed, is the stagnation of trade that scarcely a single industry is exempt from it, and to intensify this calamitous condition of affairs an early winter, which bids fair to be unusually severe, has set in. All these circumstances – the unsettled state of foreign affairs, the failures, and the depression of trade – have brought about an amount of distress for which to find parallel instances we must go back to the cotton famine as regards Lancashire, and

Lt-Gen Sir Drury Drury-Lowe, GCB, of Locko Park, Derbyshire, hero of the Kaffir Wars

to the year 1861 as regards the country generally. But there is a bright side to this gloomy picture. In all parts of England, Scotland, and Wales energetic efforts are being made to relieve individual destitution, and as our country is wealthy and possesses an infinite number of voluntary agencies for distributing relief, we do not fear the result. The Poor Law will provide for those who can claim its aid, while private benevolence will search out and render assistance to those who would rather starve to death than make their necessities known. Let us hope that at this season of the year – the Christmas glad festival – we may all feel more strongly the ties of our common brotherhood, and let us hope, too, that when the distress has passed away it will be found that the gulf which separates class from class has been permanently lessened. If instead of every man fighting for his own hand, which has of late been too much the animating spirit that has guided us, we learn that we are members of one great family, in which every one is bound to do his best for the benefit of the whole, the Christmas of 1878 will be remembered as having taught a lesson which will bring in its trail unspeakable blessings.

A Child's Christmas Eve

ALISON UTTLEY

Alison Uttley (1884–1976) was born Alison Taylor at Castle Top Farm, Cromford and was educated at Bakewell Grammar School and Manchester University where she graduated as BSc. (Hons) in physics. In 1911 she married another scientist, James Uttley, who died in 1931. Mrs Uttley began writing after her husband's death and her first book appeared in 1931.

For the next forty years she wrote regularly, winning a wide reputation with her books for children, particularly the 'Little Grey Rabbit' stories. Her descriptions of country life and country people was based on her memories of childhood on a Derbyshire farm. This extract comes from Ambush of Young Days *first published in 1937 – a selection of eighteen essays.*

Then came Christmas Eve, the night of mystery, when we hung up our stockings. Outside the wind howled dismally, crying in a human voice as it swept down the chimneys, and whistled under the doors. The dark pressed against the windows, and filled the house so that I thought of the great fires in the bedrooms as watchfires to keep at bay the strange animals that might be wandering about. In the yard the dog

rattled his chain, and gave a sharp bark as he heard some distant sound of revelry across the valley.

My mother lifted a warning forefinger, whispering: 'Hark! Hark! The dogs do bark. Beggars are coming to London Town, Beggars are coming to London Town,' and, wide-eyed, we listened.

Then, in a mysterious voice, soft and low, she began her Christmas Eve poem, the story she always told us on this wonderful night.

'Twas the night before Christmas and all through the house,
Not a creature was stirring, not even a mouse,
The stockings were hung by the chimney with care,
In hopes that Saint Nicholas soon would be there!
The children were nestled all snug in their beds,
While visions of sugar plums danced in their heads.

She went on to relate how she heard a clatter on the lawn, so that she sprang from her bed and away to the window. There, under the bright moon, was a 'miniature sleigh and eight tiny reindeer!'

We listened, clutching her fingers, scarce breathing lest we should miss any of the words we knew so well – the queer words like 'miniature', whose meaning I did not know, and never asked, and 'sugar plums', which I thought were dangling red plums dipped in the sugar bowl. There was no doubt of the truth of the story, for my mother had seen it all. Good Santa Claus, too! Our spirits were uplifted as we thought of the ancient saint who even as we sat there was speeding from the icy North with a cargo of presents for all the children on earth.

Sometime in the night he would pull up those eight antlered steeds on our own snow-covered lawn, tie them to the boles of the fir-trees, and then come down our chimney,

'There, under the bright moon was a miniature sleigh and eight tiny reindeer' by C.F. Tunnicliffe

without waking a soul. He was an angel; it was one of the miracles on the Holy Night when the Infant Christ was born, when great things happen.

After leaving our gifts he would go off to other houses in the villages, over the hills to the many valleys, to cottage and castle, to children we had never seen, bearing toys for the rich and poor, fine toys for the rich, smaller ones for the poor. I had no feeling of inequality, it was the universality of this celestial visit which affected me the most, that Santa Claus should forget no one, even the poorest child.

I lay in bed, in the soft bosom of the great feather mattress, watching the shadows play their nightly game on the ceiling, as the fire shot up the chimney with a quick roar and crackle of sparks. At the foot of the bed hung my limp stocking waiting for something to happen. Children at school said Santa Claus was your own father and mother. It wasn't true, it couldn't be true! There was the Christmas poem, with its ring

of truth, and I had a Christmas card of long ago, showing two children asleep in bed, their empty stockings at the foot, like mine. When I held it to the lamp, Santa Claus appeared leaning over, with a sackful of toys. Would they paint that if it were not true? Or were they deceived, too? Was this only a beautiful story like the floor of heaven?

The warm bed enfolded me, luring me to sleep. Dreams of a bulging stocking and a big fairy-tale book fluttered before my eyes. I was just nine years old, an important number, surely a magical age, the last of the single figures, and now I should find everything out.

The shadows leapt higher than ever as a piece of wood fell with a crash in the fire, and I sprang up in alarm. Sounds came from below the window, muffled steps, and my father's laugh as he led the barking dogs to the stable. It was the waits with their lanterns and hymn-books, their fiddles and flutes. Someone plucked the string of his fiddle, a voice gave out a note, and the words began soft and thin, then gathering force.

'Lead kindly light, amid the encircling gloom, Lead thou me on.' The voices rose and fell in the glittering air, and the frosty stars twinkled through the branches of the fir-trees. I stared at the fire, listening to the sounds sighing through the room, filling it with music which seemed to be part of the shadows. The tune changed, my father had asked for a revival song, something to stir the pulses, and bring heaven near. The words came uncertain and weak, only one man knew them, but his voice soared over the others, guiding and leading them on.

Oh! think of the home over there,
By the side of the River of Life,
Where the saints all immortal and fair,
Are robed in their garments of white –

he sang, and the faltering voices followed till he reached the chorus and then a mighty rush of song filled the air, beating over the stables, over the farmhouse, away into that great vault of sparkling winter sky:

> Over there! Over there!
> Oh, think of the home over there!

they sang, and their voices swept upward and outward, away to that implacable blue sky which, my schoolmaster said, went on for ever and ever.

Long after they had finished, when 'While shepherds watched' and 'Come all ye faithful', and 'Hark the herald angels' had been sung, and the party had entered the dining-room for elderberry wine and hot mince pies, I heard the refrain beating like a challenge through my mind, echoing through the air, flying away through the vast empty spaces towards the Milky Way.

'Over there! Over there! Oh, think of the home over there!' it rang, plaintive, questioning, like a cry from the world's heart.

I would find out. I would understand. My mind leapt swiftly as the flames. The sense of immortality filled my being, and I flung out my arms, eyes wide open, listening, and waiting for some answer.

A Memory of the Last Squire of Calke Abbey

ROSSLYN ST CLAIR

Every pew is filled with people well-wrapped against the cold, their faces falteringly lit by wavering candles in the little church on a knoll in the old deer park. The choir is in good voice as they sing out the old carols – and so are the villagers. Then the Squire moves from his pew to the lectern to read the lesson. Around him are hatchments and marble monuments to his long-dead ancestors.

The time was Christmas 1990, but this very old-fashioned and very English scene might have been in 1690 or 1790 or 1890 – only the clothes give the game away. This was a sad landmark in the story of the great house lying below in the little valley, for it was the last time that the Squire of Calke would attend the Christmas carol service which he had started and which had, in all too short a time, become a tradition.

Mr Henry Harpur-Crewe, the last Squire of Calke, inherited great estates from his bachelor brother including the vast house which was in poor condition for various reasons, not least the Second World War. Everyone knows that Calke Abbey was a sleeping beauty – a 'time capsule' as the

The church in the park of Calke Abbey where the Carol Services are held

newspapers always described it. The Harpur-Crewe family often scorned the outside world and in particular the worst aspects of the twentieth century. They never threw anything away and spent much of their time in their own wide demesnes. The last bride to have been brought to Calke was in 1875.

When 'Mr Henry' as he was known, inherited, everything changed. Thanks to him the house and some land passed to the National Trust who took on the gargantuan task of

restoration, the Squire keeping a corner for himself. The great house came into its own once again. From being a place of mystery which few people had had the privilege of seeing, it almost became open house; for the Squire, once a shy, retiring person, now revelled in it all and liked nothing better than entertaining and being entertained. In 1990 he became High Sheriff of Derbyshire and enjoyed every minute. The huge party he gave in the Abbey will long be remembered by those fortunate enough to have been there.

A High Church and Queen's man, Mr Harpur-Crewe began and maintained throughout his short reign at Calke the annual Christmas carol service. His friend Canon Paul Miller, who also acted as his High Sheriff's Chaplain, would conduct the service and afterwards all would repair through the darkness of the park to the enormous house, beckoning and ablaze with light, there to be plied with hot punch, mince pies and other good things as guests of the Squire.

The 1990 carol service was the last one in which the Squire was involved. He died suddenly while walking on his own moorland in November 1991.

Now yet one more of England's links with its traditional past has been broken. All who knew Henry will never forget his unique personality, his sense of fun, his kindness and his amiability. Christmas in this part of Derbyshire will never be the same . . .

Christmas in a Derbyshire Village

GARTH CHRISTIAN

*Garth Christian (*c. 1920–66*) was a son of the Revd F.E. Christian, Vicar of Riddings, Derbyshire and a descendant of Admiral Sir Hugh Cloberry Christian (1747–98) Naval C-in-C the Cape of Good Hope. His brother, Mr Roy Christian, is a well-known writer and broadcaster and an authority on Derbyshire.*

Mr Christian, who was a chronic invalid, taught himself how to be a writer and was the author of a number of books including Where No Birds Sing *and* Tomorrow's Countryside. *He was also a teacher and a lecturer on natural history and conservation. The Derbyshire village he is describing is probably Stanley, where he lived for a number of years.*

It really began too early. For Christmas is best reserved for the last week of December when Advent is over and a strange hush falls upon the countryside. Yet every year we used to copy the action of the Derby shopkeepers who announced '*Only* One Hundred and Fifty Days to Christmas . . . only One Hundred Days . . . only Ten Days . . . only . . .'

All of which made our neighbour furious. For he was a

farmer of the old-fashioned kind whose boyhood had been spent before 1870, the year when 'new-fangled laws about kids going to school' had been introduced. Half the troubles of the modern world he blamed on to education. In former days, he used to argue, men had obeyed the rhythm of the changing seasons, never upsetting the weather by 'putting-on the clocks,' nor holding harvest festival services while sodden stooks of wheat paraded in the rain. Christmas with its mummers and its carolling was confined to a short break of a day or so which was all that people could afford.

Then came the new law making it compulsory for boys to stay at school till they were twelve, a harsh, unjust law, he called it, hard on the parents and painful to the children who were better working in the fields than learning fancy writing in the classroom. They were happier ploughing and hedging and thinning the copses than learning Christmas carols through the weeks of late November.

For no sooner was this new law introduced, he argued, than the Christmas season grew by many weeks. Did not these school-teachers instruct their children to write letters to imaginary friends explaining what happened on the first Christmas Day – as early as mid-November? Before December was more than a day or two old, did they not set their young charges cutting out garlands for the Christmas Party and rehearsing a simple play for the same occasion? Did they not start talking Christmas, planning Christmas, preparing for Christmas even before the last smoke from Guy Fawkes bonfires had blown away?

This policy of the school authorities was simply inviting the young to grow unruly, he used to say, for bad behaviour is the sequel to excitement. Worse, it made life harder for the parents who preferred to postpone Christmas planning – and especially Christmas spending – for as long as possible.

It was not surprising, then, that the children failed to visit his house when carolling in the first dark days of December. Everybody went to the Vicarage, of course, for the parson was immensely rich. (Did he not enjoy an income of £400 a year which enabled him to employ two maids and half a gardener?) Nor were the cottages of the mining folk missed for each householder usually rewarded the carol singers with an orange or an apple or a few caramels. The blacksmith, the cobbler and the infants' school-mistress had even been known to pay twopence and threepence to a trio of young carol singers. Indeed, only 'gaffer's' garden gate remained shut throughout these weeks of December, for all the carol singers agreed that headmasters are best neither seen nor heard.

Do carol singers of today find the same ration of fun in their tour of the village? I believe the modern child expects – and invariably receives – full trade union rates for the job when he goes carol singing, and a reward of two jujubes or a halfpenny – which is all we used to get – might promptly cause a sit-down strike.

Perhaps the youngsters of today would see equal cause for offence in the simple Christmas gifts we used to enjoy. For the days of my Derbyshire boyhood were spent at a time when poverty burdened many a village home and he was a rich man who could buy his boy a bicycle. Yet thanks to the ingenuity of the poorest parents, there were no children who did not enjoy a few presents. There was always an orange and an apple at the bottom of every stocking optimistically suspended at the end of every bed; there might even be a tiny doll or a toy motor-car as well as a piece of string and a cardboard box. For the imaginative child makes good use of the simplest of gifts. How well I recall the squire's son who turned aside from his expensive toy train, ignored his bright new cycle and scorned his precious books while he and a friend unrolled a ball of string with which they 'wired the house for electricity'. This

The village of Stanley

game whose only equipment had cost a few coppers kept them happy throughout a Christmas weekend.

Even though our farmer-neighbour was right and Christmas did begin too early, there was no limit to the atmosphere of excitement that marked those last days before the climax of the long Christmas season. Who will ever forget the thrill of the postman's coming with Christmas cards rich in robins in the snow – usually and inaccurately shown in triplicate or even quadruplicate – and bearing the words 'Hearty Good Wishes for Christmas' outlined in heaped letters of mince pies, plum puddings and steaming turkeys?

Though only a small boy, I realised that the choosing of Christmas cards was a craft, perhaps even a fine art, for how dreadful it is to send a fox-hunting scene to one who prefers

the pursuit of those who hunt; how fearful to offend a staunch bird-protectionist with a curlew-shooting scene, or the lover of Picasso with a picture by Birkett Foster. Worse, how frightful to post a Picasso to one who believes that no good art has appeared since 'The Monarch of the Glen' was painted. Even more grim is the discovery that we have failed to post any Christmas cards to the people who have sent to us. I do not think my family was the only one to wonder as Christmas dawned how many enemies they had made by mismanaging this season of peace and goodwill.

Fortunately, these sombre thoughts would usually be forgotten as there came a thundering knock at the door. It might be the gamekeeper with a brace of partridge from the squire, or the doctor's gardener with a load of logs. In a moment the horrors of Christmas would be swamped by its deeper joys as neighbour gave to neighbour, friend welcomed friend, and we became increasingly aware of the family feeling of intimacy that united – and also often divided – our Derbyshire village.

For families do not always agree; indeed, there is no better way of making enemies than to marry your neighbour or your cousin. And that is what the people of my home village have been doing for generations. When the front door burst open on Christmas Eve and the mummers appeared, we knew that St George was first cousin to Beelzebub – waiting outside for his cue; the doctor's second cousin we knew to be Bold Slasher; and Little Devil Doubt who threatened to sweep us all out claimed to possess 75 cousins of whom 58 lived in the village.

Hence our quarrels; hence occasional outbursts of ill-natured gossip. Hence too our sense of intimacy with each other, for in a land where every man knows the worst of his neighbour, there is nothing to hinder the growth of what we used to call 'warmth.' No man in my home village ever indulged in artificial niceness.

My companions among the village boys quarrelled and became firm friends and quarrelled again and our elders did the same, for are not men mere boys in long trousers?

But on Christmas Day we adjourned to church after a breakfast of pork-pie – and Christmas Day without pork-pies would have seemed like an eggless Easter – with all quarrels but one forgotten. For this was the season of peace and goodwill and even the robin singing in a holly bush seemed to us to be rejoicing in the great day – though the more scientific observers of today might say he was warning his neighbour to 'clear off.'

And 'clear-off' is just what our Christmas-hating neighbour used to do even as we began to sing 'Christians, Awake'. For he had long enjoyed a fierce war with the choirmaster. Every Sunday the farming neighbour went to church; every Sunday he waited for the choir to walk out of the vestry; and every Sunday when the choir-master was with them – and he usually was – the farmer would seize his hymn book, his prayer book, his coat and hat and stride out of church.

Christmas Day brought no variation from the weekly procedure. 'Heaven's whole orb, with Alleluias rang,' shouted the choir as they reached their stalls, 'God's highest glory was their anthem still, Peace upon earth, and unto men goodwill.' And as the sound died away before the next verse began, we would hear the click of the churchyard gate as the farmer tramped home to his fireside.

At the time we all took his habit for granted, counting it as normal as the rising and setting of the sun. It was only the other day that I realised its quaintness, as a member of my family said: 'You ought to mention it in a Christmas article.'

But of course, I would not dream of doing so.

A Gardener's Christmas

ROBERT AUGHTIE

Robert Aughtie started his working life as a gardener at Chiswick House near London. He was employed by the 6th Duke of Devonshire who later brought him up to Derbyshire where he worked under Joseph Paxton at Chatsworth during the construction of the Great Conservatory.

Aughtie kept an illustrated diary, part of which has recently been published in a beautiful edition. The extract below relates to Christmas 1848.

December 1848

22nd – Friday – Walked to Bakewell with Littlewood and Barton – called on Mr Bradbury and paid him a bill – returned home with Barton – a most delightful night.

23rd – Saturday – The ice-house was filled today by George's men.

24th – Sunday – A fine dry frosty morning – went to Chaple – Mr Spencer pr. Dined with the Bradbury's – went with Mr B Sen. to Longston Chaple – my first appearance there. It was

a very bleak cold walk – returned to Bradbury's to tea – found them to be a very agreeable set of folks – went to chaple – while there, it commenced snowing – was accompanied home by William Milward and Mr Sedding – called on W. Bland – we agreed to go to the Romish chaple at Hassop, at midnight, to hear high mass – we accordingly started about 1/2 past 10 p.m. – had a most delightful walk there – called on Hiddulph, but found he was gone – there was not so many people at the chaple as I expected – Bland and Milward was much pleased – on our way home, we went to Baslow, to hear the carolists who had then just turned out – returned home. Bland went home with me and had some breakfast – we then went out to the carol singers – after going through the village with them, we returned home about 1/2 past 5. William and I then went to bed together – this is about the pleasantist Christmas eve that I ever spent. The fine clear night and the novelty of the scene was, to me, quite delightful.

25th – Monday – Christmas day – after two hours and a half sleep, we got up at eight – we had some breakfast together – went to the Church, there not being any service at the chaple – dined with Mrs Wallace, off the beef given by the Duke. While at dinner, William Milward called on me to take a walk – we walked a little in the Park and looked over the farm yard – paid a visit to his father – had been invited to the Sedding's, to spend the evening – went there to tea and had tea there, but left directly after, as he had to go to Ashford with the school children, to sing the carol to Mr Cavendish. Went with W. Milward to Baslow – called on his sister at the parsonage – we then went to church with them – my first appearance there. Mr Barker pr. a very dull spiritless sermon – returned home – called at the Milwards – had a little chat with them – then went home to bed – this is how I spent my Christmas day of '49. [*sic*] – throughout the whole of the day

One of Robert Aughtie's own illustrations for his diary

it was miserably damp and misty, the beautiful dry frost of last night having disappeared.

26th – Tuesday to 30th – Saturday – Was rather unwell the week, perhaps owing to the weather, which was very mild and damp – on Thursday there was a ball at the Rutland Arms tavern, Bakewell – on Friday I received a letter from Emily containing 'The Comic Almanack' wrote a letter to her this Saturday evening.

31st – Sunday – A fine frosty morning with snow on the ground – went to chaple – Mr Spencer pr. – returned to dinner – was accompanied by Thomas Bland, in the evening, to Chaple – was badly attended both morn and night. This is the last day of the old year – with me it has ended better than it began.

Christmas Visitors

The following is a letter addressed to the Derbyshire Times *on 9 January 1875.*

Owing, I surmise, to the hard weather keeping so many persons out of regular employment, our Derbyshire Christmas visitors in the shape of morris dancers, carol singers, &c., appear to be unusually frequent. I live on an unfrequented road, in quite a small hamlet, some six or seven miles from the county town, and the following is my experience in chronological order –

(1) Christmas Eve, 6 p.m. Six Morris Dancers, youths bedecked with old finery and scraps of paper, who danced and stamped about in the snow without much rhyme or reason to the music of an accordian, concluding with a Christy Minstrel melody.

(2) Christmas Eve, 6.30 p.m. A troop of Mummers, or Guizors as I think they are more usually called in Derbyshire, five in number, who entered the kitchen and acted a short play, the characters being St George, Slasher, the Doctor, and Old Bet. St George and Slasher engaged in mortal combat, when the latter is killed. He is restored to life by the Doctor, and the three are then joined by Old Bet, when they break into a song which concludes the performance. The performers were dressed in various fantastic garbs, profusely ornamented with scraps of coloured paper, and the two knights armed with tin swords. The fifth member of the troop appeared to be a super-numerary and money-holder. The dialogue was

vigorous and quaint in language though pronounced without much energy or distinctness. As far as I could gather it much resembled the opening portions of the old Christmas play of St George that is often acted in the West Riding of Yorkshire under the title of 'the Peace Egg'. I am hoping shortly to secure one of the *dramatis personæ* of this troop, and if I should be fortunate enough to procure from him their version of this play I will gladly communicate it to your columns.

(3) Christmas Eve, 7.30 p.m. A band of Carol-singers, four men and a woman. The 'Carols' were all hymns of the most approved and newest type – all of them, I believe, to be found in 'Hymns Ancient and Modern' not a single real carol amongst them, not even 'God rest ye, merry gentlemen'.

(4) Christmas day. In the evening came five children singing hymns.

(5) December 26th, 12.30 p.m. Three men playing somewhat dolefully on three brass instruments 'Christians, Awake', and other sacred melodies.

(6) December 26th, 3 p.m. A troop of seven morris dancers, but dressed more after the fashion of nigger minstrels than the traditional mummers, an effect which was increased by five of them having blackened their faces. The tallest and most ungainly of the party was caparisoned as a woman. To the sound of a concertina they danced burlesque waltzes and quadrilles, but happily they did not possess that French agility which leads to cancan steps. This incongruous medley of a performance was concluded by a 'walk round' of the whole company, singing, with more vigour than accuracy, the very unseasonable and inappropriate glee, 'In a little boat we row'.

(7) December 28th, 11 a.m. Four young men, with music book in hand, sang glees and anthems with much precision and good effect. This band represented Christian harmony in a double sense, for I learnt on inquiry that two were members of a Church choir, and the two other members of a Baptist and

Independent choir respectively. But here again were no Christmas carols.

I wonder if the experience of any other of your Derbyshire readers has been wider this season than mine; and I hope they will communicate such experiences to your columns, especially if relative to the plays acted by mummers, which are so fast dying out in almost every county in the kingdom. I cannot grumble at the fewness of my visitors, but I missed one pleasant sound that it has formerly been my lot to hear at Christmas-tide in our county, – I allude to the hand-bell ringers, and I am sure that if some of the singers will have learnt one or two good old-fashioned carols by next season, they will run a fair chance of still further loosening the purse-strings of

AN OLD FOGY.

A Crimean Christmas

The Crimean War (1854–6) had strong Derbyshire connections. Florence Nightingale herself lived at Lea Hurst, a country house not far from Matlock, and Lt-Gen Sir Drury Curzon Drury-Lowe of Locko Park was a young officer serving in the Crimea and was at the Siege of Sebastopol. He had a subsequent brilliant military career as an outstanding cavalier commander in the 17th Lancers.

During Christmas, 1855, as the columns of *The Derby Mercury* show, the celebrations at Derby as elsewhere were

overshadowed by the Crimean War. But it was a better year than 1854: the military situation had improved, and more was being done for the welfare of the troops. 'Sebastopol', the name 'which twelve months ago blanched many a cheek, and saddened all', would in 1855 be a motif in the Christmas decorations. Some of the soldiers were home, and the *Mercury* forecast: 'What roars of laughter there will be over the story of the cold pudding sent out, and carved by the soldiers in its cloth and with a rusty bayonet! the Turkish-made pudding prepared according to an English recipe in which all was mentioned except the superabundant cloth, the pudding being served in a jug, and looking like so much badly-made gruel!'

The *Mercury* had well over a column, in the very smallest type, about the 'Christmas Show of Fat Meat, &., in Derby'. And James Sutton, Esq., of Shardlow Hall, had with his usual kind consideration slaughtered a fine cow which was distributed in proportionate quantities amongst the poor. The inmates of the Derby County Lunatic Asylum had their treat again as usual, on Christmas Eve.

George Herrick of Hilton came to Derby and celebrated too well: he was found lying in a drunken sleep in Babington-Lane at 2.15 in the morning. Taken to the lock-up he asked for his sister, saying he had brought her with him to take care of him. (Laughter in court; fine five shillings and 'expenses'.)

But not all was joviality and the festive spirit. 'A Burgess' wrote a neat and thin-lipped letter to the *Mercury*: 'Sir – Will any of your readers be pleased to explain to us, unlearned in municipal law, whether the Town Council of Derby desire any special exemption from the directions of the 52nd section of the Municipal Corporations Act, regulating the filling-up of vacancies in their body. And if those regulations are in force, it is to be hoped they will at once proceed to carry them into effect, rather than invite a compulsory proceeding by mandamus'.

Derbyshire's own Crimean heroine – Florence Nightingale

Locko Park's picture gallery, Christmas 1990

Perhaps, though, even 'A Burgess' relaxed: say at the grand evening concert arranged by the Anemoic Union, or at one of the several balls advertised in the *Mercury*. At worst, if still troubled with his liver, he could have gone to Mr Smedley's hydropathic establishment at Matlock: 'Pecuniary emolument not an object. Mild treatment', the advertisements ran. Who knows, hydropathy might have been capable of inducing a Christmas spirit.

A Closing Memory of Lord Harrington

BEATRICE HOLDEN

Beatrice Holden (d. 1949) was born Beatrice Paget, the fifth daughter of Herbert Byng Paget, of Darley House, Darley Dale, Derbyshire.

A dedicated huntswoman she was, in the words of her brother Guy, 'blooded on the borders of the Meynell and Quorn in the great days of Tom Firr'. She was a competent and fearless rider and was also a poet. Some of her work appeared in Horse and Hound *under the pseudonym 'Peccavi'. This poem, with its introduction, comes from 'They're Away!' In 1900 she married Wilfred Holden, a Warwickshire Squire.*

The Earl of Harrington

HIS LAST HUNT – 'IT'S HOME, GENTLEMEN.'

These verses were inspired by a letter to the author from the Baroness Burton, of Rangemore, Burton-on-Trent, an extract from which reads as follows: 'You do not mention, however, in your article on Lord Harrington a very curious incident, viz., that which happened after his Lordship's death. He left in his will that his hounds were to hunt the first convenient day after his funeral at Elvaston. Fred Earp duly took hounds out in accordance with his Master's wishes, but only a few others were present. The pack found in the Policies, and ran straight to Lord Harrington's grave, where they checked. Fred Earp then remarked, 'Well, gentlemen, I am going home; His Lordship has called his hounds.'

Said Wistful to Wanderer, 'It's a lovely hunting morn,'
Said Wanderer to Wistful, 'Hush! I fancy that's the horn;
I believe I see his Lordship at the far end on the grey,

And it's very strange, because I thought they'd taken him
away.
Fred Earp was telling Keeper that his Lordship's gone to rest,
And he'd lost the finest Master, and the greatest, and the best;
Yet I seem to hear him calling (for now I cannot see him),
Have a care, Wanderer! Gently! Do you think it *can* be him?'

And as Wanderer spoke to Wistful a big grey fox broke
covert,
And Fred's voice came o'er the breeze with 'Lui in, my lads,
yoi over!'
And said Wisful unto Wanderer, 'Why don't he blow his
horn?
He doesn't seem to notice that a big grey fox has gone.'
'And *that's* very strange,' said Wanderer, 'and I've simply got
to go.'
They topped the fence together for they'd heard a tally-ho-o-o!
It seemed to them they *had* to go – they hadn't any choice,
'Cos of 'Forrard! – Forrard! – Forrard!' in their own dear
Master's voice,

'. . . a big grey fox broke covert'

Elvaston Castle

They threw their tongues and raced away, heads up, sterns down they flew,
His Lordship was a'calling them – they knew! – they knew! they knew!
Five and twenty couple frantic, straining, fleet,
A sheet could have covered them (Ah, yes! a winding sheet;)
Five and thirty minutes up to the Golden Gates,*
Straight as a line to the churchyard, 'where,' said they, 'his Lordship waits.'
There was never a sign of the big grey fox – the grass was trampled and pressed
Where yesterday the best-loved man in the Midlands was laid to rest.

* The big gates at the main avenue leading to Elvaston Castle have always been known as the 'Golden Gates'.

Fred whispered to the solemn field
Bare-headed amongst the mounds,
'Gentlemen, I am taking them home;
His Lordship has called his hounds.'

Two Cheers for Christmas

The following is an extract from the Derbyshire Advertiser *of 27 December 1878.*

This gloomy columnist compiled a tale of woe just before Christmas 1878 on page 93. Here, he reports in the same style after the celebrations are over.

Christmas has again been celebrated at Derby with some, at least, of the customary rejoicings. As we said last week, there were one or two circumstances which militated against the universal feeling of rejoicing with which this season of the year is generally hailed. Only a few days ago, the death of the Princess Alice* cast a widespread gloom over us, and we are as yet, so to speak, under the shadow of that great calamity. Then we have been suffering from a period of commercial

* The Grand Duchess of Hesse, Queen Victoria's second daughter who died on 14 December 1878.

depression of exceptional severity and duration. Added to these misfortunes, we have had for some two or three weeks past a very severe frost, which – though pleasant to skaters, bent on pleasure – has been a serious matter for persons engaged in building operations, etc., and for the workmen and labourers dependent for their livelihood on undertakings of this character.

In spite of all these drawbacks, much has been done in Derby towards the joyful celebration of Christmas. The shops have put on holiday attire, and their windows have been decked out to the best possible advantage. The churches have been decorated with varying degrees of ornateness and beauty, and the customary Christmastide services have been held in them. And something more than the customary services too,

Christmas in Derby earlier this century. Roome's, the famous fishmonger and poulterer, is still one of the city's most popular shops and still in the ownership of the same family

for midnight services on Christmas Eve – a new feature in Derby, or rather an old feature revived – were held in two or three churches. At St Michael's there was a midnight service consisting of Christmas hymns and carols, interspersed with addresses; and at St Peter's, there was a choral celebration of the Holy Communion at midnight, followed by Christmas carols. Even the Nonconformist places of worship – or some of them at least – observed the festival. At Friar-gate Chapel, on Sunday last (as recorded elsewhere) there was a special Service of Song, and one of a somewhat similar nature was held at the Osmaston-road Baptist Chapel on Christmas Day.

On Christmas Eve the 'waits' or carol singers pursued their usual midnight avocations, and the choirs and bands attached to several places of worship went round and serenaded their principal friends and supporters. In one way, Christmas was not observed this year, and as the custom was better kept by the breach than the observance, we do not regret the circumstance. There were none of those 'Christmas drawings' at public-houses and elsewhere, which used to be so prevalent, but are now put down by the police on the ground that they have been declared illegal by the magistrates. Madame Mary Cummings' concert has been the great musical feature of the week, and then we have the Choral Union concert to look forward to.

At the Corn Exchange, the 'Derby Pantomine' opened with a fair degree of acclaim, and it seems likely to meet with the success which its enterprising promoters deserve. Skating on the ice has of course been one of the principal sources of enjoyment in this frosty weather; and for those who still prefer skating on rollers, the managers of the rink have provided special attractions. Christmas Day and the day following (Boxing Day) have been observed almost as a general holiday in the town – that is to say, the banks and most of the places of business have been closed. The men engaged in the

locomotive department at the Midland Railway Works are having a week's holiday, but in the carriage department, where there is a comparative pressure, less holiday has been given.

There is not much to add to this record of Christmas doings, for we cannot chronicle home rejoicings or cross the sacred limits of 'our own firesides'. The poor have not been neglected – many 'doles' have been distributed, the soup kitchens have been opened, and the liberal stream of bounty has flowed forth freely.

A Bit of Derbyshire Dialect

ROBERT MURRAY GILCHRIST

Robert Murray Gilchrist was born at Heeley, Sheffield in 1867 but spent most of his short life (he died in 1917) in Derbyshire writing stories and novels with a Derbyshire background. Gilchrist knew several contemporary literary giants such as Galsworthy, Shaw, Housman, and Arnold Bennett who described his stories as 'technically brilliant'. His books include Peakland Faggot; Honeysuckle Rouge; Damosel Croft *and* Natives of Milton *– a story about Eyam. He often made much of the broad Derbyshire dialect now much diluted as in this extract from his story* The Last Posset.

'Et shall be a posset – a Kirsmas posset i' harvest time. Little else but posset hes been drunk aat o' thee i' my livin' mem'ry. An' et mun be th' strongest posset as thaa'st held i' thy belly for mony a long year. Gin i' et, an' rum, an' nutmegs, an' cloves, an' ginger. I wunna hev no milk – a gill o' cream wi' lump sugar's th' best. An' a raand o' toast to soften et.' She took a little brass saucepan from the rack and poured in the ale and set it over the clear heart of the fire. One by one she dropped in the spices, and when the contents had begun to simmer, she moved the pan to the hob and cut a slice of bread. This she toasted until it was of a uniform straw colour; then she broke it into the posset jug and soaked it with cream. The ale sent a pungent aroma through the room.

A Victorian Christmas in Derby

W.A. RICHARDSON

The following is taken from Richardson's Citizens Derby *published in 1949. The author was a lecturer at Derby Technical College.*

Assemblies went out of fashion. Theatres and concerts were less popular in the forties. Oratorios in aid of the Infirmary hardly paid expenses. Houses had become more comfortable, whilst books, newspapers and magazines were abundant, so people entertained at home. Round games, cards and informal

dances were popular. Yet the town was soon to have 'The Star Music-hall.' When Jenny Lind sang in Derby 1,200 people heard her. Thackeray lectured before the Mayor on George III, and Charles Dickens read bits out of *Martin Chuzzlewit.* More to the liking of the people, maybe, was Blondin's performance on the tight-rope, for in spite of a wet day a great crowd watched him in the Arboretum.

Christmas was *the* season of festivity. Employers entertained their work-people. Mr E. Noon always gave 250 pints of Burton beer to 250 old people, says the *Derbyshire Advertiser.* The Christmas tree, just brought to England from Germany by Prince Albert, was soon found in every Derby home. On Twelfth Night there used to be a fête in the Drill Hall. A Christmas ball, in which about 200 people joined, used to be held at the Assembly Rooms.

Travelling players gave shows either in the Market Place or in the courtyard of the Virgin Inn. Did they play anything of

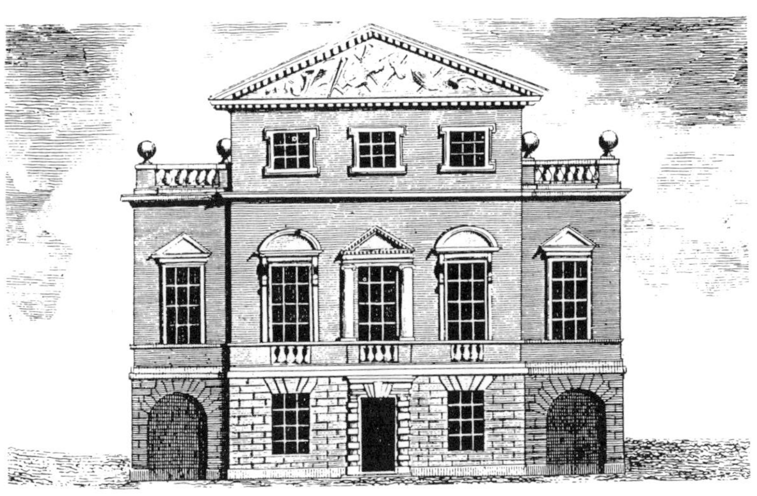

The Assembly Rooms in Derby Market Place. They were demolished in the 1970s

Shakespeare's here? 'Mummers' – men and boys in grotesque disguises – used to go from house to house at Christmastide playing an ancient farce, for which they were given ale, cakes and a few pence. The play was called *The Old Tup*, and is thought to survive in the burlesque ballad called the 'Derby Ram':

When I was going to Derby, Sir,
  All on a Market Day,
I saw the finest Ram, Sir,
  That ever fed on hay.
The Ram was fat behind, Sir,
  The Ram was fat before,
The Ram was ten yards high, Sir,
  Indeed he was no more.

A Boxing Day Entertainment

An anonymous article which appeared in Derbyshire Life and Countryside *in January 1965.*

Boxing Day morning is surely a suitable time for what has now become an annual event in Derbyshire – the Raft Race between members of the Derby and Matlock Sub-Aqua Clubs.

The River Derwent, on which it takes place, is one of the most picturesque and historic stretches of water in England.

The course, about three-and-a-half miles in length, starts at Matlock Bridge and finishes at Cromford Bridge. Last year the race was covered by the Press and filmed for television – giving it the kudos of national interest.

By eleven o'clock on Boxing Day a cheerful crowd has gathered at the starting point, and the competitors line up in pairs in the car park adjoining the river. They have given considerable thought to their apparel for this important occasion. Any form of dress over diving suits is permitted and they vie with one another to achieve sartorial originality. A wide range of eye-catching and bizarre clothing is to be seen. Morning coat and top hat, for instance, give a formal, elegant, Ascot-like air to the event; pyjamas or nightshirts, though not so dignified, are colourful and homely, while football jerseys add to the sporting, competitive side of the affair and battle dress and peak cap contribute a smart, military look.

The female entrants do not allow themselves to be outdone in dress, of course, and appear chic and up-to-date in vivid blouses and summery straw hats.

Powered or mechanical means of propulsion are not allowed. The most common type of raft used is that made of roped-together petrol cans or a 'scaffolding' of rubber inner tubes, which may be propelled by oars or paddles. The less orthodox in design they are, the better.

As the starting pistol is fired the contenders have to run down a slope of twenty feet to where the rafts await them, either floating at the water's edge or staked in midstream, and as each raft is boarded by its well-dressed couple, the race begins.

Sporting people among the spectators who have braved the winter weather in the hope of seeing an orthodox, orderly race will be disappointed. Nothing about this race – not even the start – can be called orderly. The only comparison with that famous event, the Derby, comes before the start when rafts are

Colourful Raft Race competitors approaching Matlock Bridge

apt to be carried away by fast-running currents like impatient and fractious racehorses at the starting-post. This makes for chaos and since the first raft away is temporarily in a slightly advantageous position, there is more than a little jostling for place.

For the first ten yards a good current favours light rafts, while the heavy ones tend to lag. But eventually they are all away and then it is anybody's guess as to who will win, as many underhand methods of sabotage come into play among the crews. Indeed, those words which meant so much in one's youth – 'the honour of the school' and 'fair play' are forgotten. All manner of diabolical instruments are produced at appropriate moments for the purpose of severing ropes, slashing rubber tubing and doing as much damage as possible to rival craft.

As for the course itself, it is more than a little hazardous.

Four rapids and two weirs have to be passed over, and on Boxing Day the water is generally at its highest. The weirs cause the downfall of many hopes, for the more fragile craft, bumping over them, tend to break up, leaving their crews struggling in the water. And since no competitors can hope to win unless they finish the course *on* their raft, there is constant effort to retain at least some portion of it.

Meanwhile, what of the shivering spectators? They can see the whole race, from start to finish, by walking along the river bank. Those without the energy to cover the course on foot, find vantage points which offer special thrills. Matlock's equivalent of Beecher's Brook is perhaps High Tor, where the first rapid is, or High Tor Mills where the weir has a drop of 15 feet. Masson Weir, at Arkwright's Mill, has an even greater drop.

As the last leg of the course is approached, the flagging energies of competitors revive as they sight the finishing post. Their loyal supporters, who have been shouting encouragement all along the course, add zest to their efforts. When snow is about, some young devotees will wait on bridges, to give proof of their enthusiasm by dropping large snowballs down the necks of the crews as they pass under.

All is not over when the winners have passed the post. Other gallant finishers have lost oars or paddles, or the remains of their rafts and have the utmost difficulty in reaching the bank, to the somewhat unfeeling amusement of those around.

The first two couples to reach the winning post are awarded silver trophies; the 'also rans' share in the general jubilation for winners and losers celebrate in true style afterwards. Every move, strategy and hazard, is argued over and the vagaries of the individual rafts are discussed. By unanimous vote, the continuation of this Boxing Day event is assured.

The Boxing Day Shoot

JOHN WILLIAMSON

John Williamson, born at Bradbourne in Derbyshire, has lived most of his life at Kirk Langley. He is now retired but was a frequent broadcaster, having made his first on the BBC in 1950, and contributor to local newspapers and journals covering characters and events of the last half century. He is a countryman at heart with a farming background as this account of the goings-on at a Boxing Day shoot demonstrates.

Christmas 1919 was bitterly cold, with a hard frost and covering of snow. For the Derbyshire farmer the outlook was less bleak, cattle were fetching big sums and there was a keen demand for dairy products.

Guaranteed prices for wheat, oats and milk had induced tenants to take up money to buy their farms, and Christmas was an appropriate moment to celebrate these prosperous times with the traditional Boxing Day shoot.

On the Radburne Estate large shooting parties for the gentry were held in the weeks before Christmas, when pheasants were plentiful. But on Boxing Day the order was always 'tenants only' and the main sport rabbits.

The shooting party which gathered at Tyrrel Hayes Farm, Radbourne, had come to enjoy themselves. Soon after 9.30 a.m. friends and neighbours arrived by pony and trap and greetings were exchanged in the frosty air.

Sporting characters like Dick Finney, the local butcher, and Bob Welch from the Hepnalls, Etwall, along with Frank Stretton of Butt House, Thurvaston, and Richard Archer from Wild Park, Mercaston, were warming their backsides before the kitchen fire.

In the yard the Revd Jack Wardale of Dalbury Rectory, had arrived with John Massey from Rook Hills Farm. A smart governess-cart drove up with Richard Wood from Silverhill, accompanied by Sam Smith of The Potlocks Farm.

Tommy Ault and Jack Thornhill from Langley Common were waiting in a carthovel with a box of ferrets and spade.

Conditions were ideal for rabbiting – bright and still on the frozen snow. Guns tucked under their arms, this little

'Guns tucked under their arms ...'

gathering headed for the Birchwood, where a tiny stream ran through bracken towards Dalbury church.

Sam Clowes, from Park Farm, with William Clifford, joined them by the 'Rough', and nodded to indicate that rabbits were 'at home'. Boxing Day was a lighthearted occasion – a sort of 'stand back and shoot affair', with a ferret to bolt a few rabbits.

The exercise helped to work off the effects of too much Christmas dinner and generated another good appetite for the evening meal.

Spitting on his hands, Jack Thornhill took out a jill ferret, which blinked in the daylight, sniffed briefly and disappeared down a hole. A rabbit emerged under a sycamore stump. There goes another!

Two shots broke the silence. The ferret worked back and forth along the bank. A shot from Sam Archer caught a rabbit leaving a bolt-hole beneath a tuft of grass. A couple more climbed the ditch and Frank Stretton got both.

For half-an-hour rabbits were dodging in and out of burries and sporadic shots cracked the silence. Seven more were stopped in their tracks and the sportsmen looked pleased.

While each man took a large sip from a pocket-flask, Tommy Ault paunched the rabbits and the Parson spread them out on the frozen grass, carefully 'hocking' their hind legs.

He always had a thought-provoking saying on Boxing Day: 'Shooting over ferrets should be done with care – particularly after Christmas fare!'

The rabbiting party now moved on to the Trusley side of the Rough and a strong hob ferret, attached to a line, was thrust into a large hole.

Five minutes passed. Suddenly an old dog fox bolted from the bury and seven guns barked in unison. The intruder lay still.

Parson joins the Boxing Day shoot

'By God, Sam, there'll be the devil to pay for this', said Richard Wood, pretending innocence.

'You shot 'im!' Bob Welch exclaimed.

'Damned if I did – you were closer'.

Fox slaying in Radbourne was regarded as almost a crime. In days gone by 'vulpicide' could have meant instant notice to quit the tenancy.

'Gentlemen', the Revd Jack Wardale intervened, 'no word will ever reach the Master'. There was a twinkle in his eye. 'Let's call it a bonus to our Boxing Day rabbiting'. He was a good man.

Tommy Ault produced an old sack, the fox was dumped in and the neck of the bag tied securely. It was time for the trek home.

In the furthest corner of the orchard, where a clump of damson trees hid them from view, Jack Thornhill dug a deep hole and Tommy Ault dropped the sack with a sigh of relief.

'One less to bother your poultry, Sam', Mr Wardale told grandfather and the gnarled old damson tree bowed low in the breeze.

Shadowy lanterns shone from the buildings and there was a homely rattle of milk pails. Twenty-one clean, stiffened rabbits carried on a pole were a wonderful sight. But the kitchen table set out to welcome the party looked even better.

At one end Dick Finney carved the ribs of beef. At the other grandfather took his knife to a fine home-cured ham.

Mr Wardale said grace: 'For all Thy bounteous gifts and for all the great friendships we enjoy, we thank Thee, O Lord'.

At the end of the meal everyone crowded into the drawing-room for a noisy game of penny nap. In the fireglow their faces shone with contentment. Another bottle of whisky was emptied. No one actually declined, despite hollow hints to 'steady on, Sam!'

The party broke up at 10 o'clock. Lanterns were lit and wheels crunched on the frozen snow. A day-old calf blared loudly to its mother, waiting for tomorrow's dawn.

The old farmhouse looked so solid and permanent against the sky. A heavy key turning in the lock marked the end of Boxing Night.

A Victorian Christmas Miscellany

These items appeared in various Derbyshire newspapers in the last century.

CHRISTMAS GUISERS

It is customary in the Wirksworth district to indulge in a kind of theatrical performance on Christmas Eve. The actors are termed 'guisers' and are attired in 'regalia', in some cases consisting of paper adornments such as stars and high-pointed hats covered with stars. It is very entertaining to listen to these 'paper' youngsters. They perform an act in which the prominent characters are St George the Nobleman, the Doctor and a Collector who, at the close of the proceedings, hands round to all the spectators a ladle intended for subscriptions repeating, while he gathers, the following:

My father's a blacksmith
My mother's a weaver;
If you've anything to give
I'm the receiver.

The whole act is in the form of doggerel of which the above lines are an extract. The performers travel from house to house and often earn a respectable sum of money each.

A lane near Wirksworth

Latterly the 'paper' has in a great measure been discarded and instead of the former good order maintained over the sport, roughness and mischief enter largely into the game, masks being worn, faces blackened and female garments adopted by some performers. As for the doggerel it is scarcely ever used now. The appearance of some of these gangs reminds one of 'Thurkill's Host', for they are a terror to ordinary people who are often insulted by them.

ST THOMAS'S DAY

'Is the custom of "Going a-Thomasing" still kept up in the County of Derby? Well do I remember the troops of old and young women and children who went round the villages on the morning of this day and who visited all the gentlemen's houses and all the outlying farms within half-a-dozen or so miles around. They came not "by one, by two, by three" but by the score! "Please wull yo ge's a-Thomasin'?" was their cry all through the morning. In the afternoon I suppose they enjoyed the results of their enterprise. The orthodox fashion of "Going a-Thomasing" was to provide yourself with a peck bag and a two-quart tin – larger articles if you thought proper: the bag to hold the meal and apples, the tin to hold the milk. I never saw anything else to be given except meal, milk and apples in the eatable way: if any exception was, it was by giving a few pence. I am reminded that sometimes a few potatoes and an outside cut of bacon was given in place of meal and milk.

'I shall be pleased to know if this custom is still kept up and if the gifts vary in any part of Derbyshire from the particulars I have given above?'

This is from a letter to a newspaper written in the 1870s. The Editor commented: 'Thomasing still lingers in many parts of Derbyshire but we cannot hear of it assuming any

other form except pence at the present day.' The St Thomas here is St Thomas the Apostle – 'Doubting Thomas' whose feast day is December 21st.

ST THOMAS'S EVE

Derbyshire girls used to work a charm on St Thomas's Eve which had relation to their sweethearts. They used to procure a large red onion, and after peeling it stick therein nine ordinary pins, during the process saying:

Good St Thomas do me right
Send me my true love this night
In his clothes and his array
Which he weareth every day,
That I may see him in the face
And in my arms may him embrace.

Eight pins were stuck round one in the centre to which was given the name of the 'true love'. The onion was then placed under the pillow on going to bed, and the dreams of the night would be in accord with the words of the charm.

BEES SINGING ON OLD CHRISTMAS EVE

'It is yet asserted by some old people that bees emit a sound which is called "singing" at midnight on old Christmas Eve, the 6th January, commemorative of the birth of our Saviour. For many years the annual custom of listening at the hives of bees has, I believe, been entirely given up. I have heard it spoken of but I do not know anyone who has listened. For my own part I like to believe somewhat in this singing of bees

and I hope to ascertain for myself on the next old Christmas Eve if bees do not emit a sound at midnight.

I read some time ago of a gentleman who investigated this subject and he declares that the bees gave out "a solemn harmonious sound" on the night in question at midnight.'

MINCE PIES

'As many mince pies as you eat at Christmas, as many happy months you will have in the coming year' is what is said in Derbyshire. But this form of the saying is not quite correct. The twelve days from Christmas Day to Twelfth Day are the only proper days in the year on which mince pies may be eaten. One a day eaten on each of the twelve days will induce twelve happy months in the coming year! Here then is the much wished for receipt – how to be happy always. But you must not eat them at any other time in the year or you will spoil the effect.

'The shape of mince pies is another very particular matter. On no account must you make and eat *round* mince pies. Long *oval* ones are the only shaped ones allowable. Oval mince pies are intended to represent the creche or manger in which the child Christ was laid.'

Acknowledgements

I am indebted to Mr B.C. Wood the proprietor of *Derbyshire Life and Countryside* for permission to reproduce several articles and photographs which have appeared in the magazine over the last sixty years.

The items on Chatsworth are reproduced by courtesy of Her Grace the Duchess of Devonshire and Messrs Macmillan. 'A Bunch of Snowdrops' by Sir Osbert Sitwell is by courtesy of Mr Frank Magro, and the drawings that accompany it by Donald E. Green are reproduced with the artist's permission. The extracts from letters from the late Dame Edith Sitwell are reproduced by kind permission of Mr Francis Sitwell and the Sargent group of the Sitwell family is by courtesy of Sir Reresby Sitwell, Bt. The passages from Alison Uttley's *Ambush of Young Days* and the illustration by C.F. Tunnicliffe are by permission of the publishers, Faber & Faber Ltd. 'A Boxing Day Shoot' is reproduced by permission of the author Mr John Williamson. Mr and Mrs Basil Harley have allowed me to reproduce an extract and drawing from Robert Aughtie's *A Gardener at Chatsworth*. The letters of D.H. Lawrence are reproduced by courtesy of Lawrence's literary executors. Mr Ron Duggins has allowed me to use his photograph of the Raft Race.

Captain Patrick Drury-Lowe and photographer Roy Deeley gave me permission to use the picture gallery at Locko Park.

The December extract from *A Derbyshire Year* is reproduced by permission of the author Miss Elizabeth Eisenberg. 'Some Eyam Carols' and 'Some Christmas Customs and Carols' by the late Clarence Daniel are reproduced by courtesy of Mrs

Daniel. 'Christmas in a Derbyshire Village' by the late Garth Christian is reproduced by courtesy of his brother Mr Roy Christian. I am indebted to Mr Frank Rodgers for his photograph of the village of Stanley and likewise to Miss B.H. Sadler for her drawing of the old Union Workhouse at Ashbourne. Mrs Vernon D. Shaw gave permission to use her husband's photograph of Hayfield. I am indebted to Mr Maxwell Craven and the Derby Art Gallery and Museum for permission to use photographs of the Arboretum, King's Newton, Melbourne and a lane near Wirksworth. Thanks also to Robin Gibbard and Pamela Gee.

I have tried to cover all permissions, but if anyone has been left out I apologize. I would like to thank my wife who has done much of the spadework for this anthology and who read the proofs.